Advance Praise

Ernest Thompson, fondly known as Home, Homeboy, and Big Train, makes plain for us that coalition building may appear as intuitive as preparing a meal, but reminds us that it is less intuitive and more intentional and sacrificial. Through engaging glimpses of his childhood experiences and actual anecdotes from coalition building, Thompson suggests it takes a broad and inclusive approach. He points out the complexities of making intentional efforts to bring together all required ingredients and utensils to build meaningful and healthy coalitions and the challenging sacrifices that are unending. This book encourages the reader to not be complacent with injustice anywhere and to draw from their own strengths to build coalitions that work to actualize a People's Democracy rooted in universal equality.

—Rev. Dr. Anika Whitfield of Little Rock

Homeboy Came to Orange is an essential read for anyone who wants to organize for change in their towns, schools, churches or communities. It is a story that is at once inspiring, challenging, and unwavering.

—Terri Baltimore,
Director of Community Engagement,
Hill House Association

I did not realize how much Ernie Thompson had influenced my approach to public health until I reread *Homeboy Came to Orange*. Fourteen years ago, I read it as a way to understand and put into context the work of NYC RECOVERS, an organization whose goal was to promote collective recovery post the 9/11 disaster. At the time, I understood how Ernie's approach to coalition building, bringing together allies on common denominators – "We don't come together because we're Black and White, we come together because we're workers"– could be leveraged in service of my work with NYC RECOVERS, the UNIDOS Coalition, and later with CLIMB (City Life Is Moving Bodies). After rereading the book, I can clearly see Ernie's legacy in my research and practice. Ernie taught me to ground my work on what I am *for* – not what I am against – and that lesson was transformative. My work with the Center for Youth Violence Prevention transformed into youth development and neighborhood strengthening. My ideas about using harm reduction strategies to improve public spaces were not about displacing undesirable users from parks, sidewalks and streets, but rather about making room for other users and inviting people to bring their contributions to our organizational potluck. By doing so, we made positive uses and stewardship the norm and made northern Manhattan parks safer. Ernie was not only witty and strategic, but also straightforward and unapologetic. I learned from him how to respectfully disagree and challenge –isms, never in an accommodating way, but rather by infiltrating, elevating, and creating opportunities for awakening. I am a much more effective public health person because of the lessons culled from *Homeboy Came to Orange*.

—**Lourdes J Rodriguez, DrPH, Director,**
Center for Place-Based Initiatives,
Dell Medical School

Home for Ernie Thompson is the small town of Orange, N.J. Although Orange is only 2.2 square miles in size, "Homeboy's" story is filled with lessons for people living in much bigger cities. Dr. Mindy Fullilove's skilled narrative is a lens through which she uncovers the embedding context, diverse perspectives and interpersonal episodes shared today by many people struggling for justice and equity on Main Streets and in towns and cities across our country.

—**William Morrish, Professor of Urban Ecologies, Parsons School of Design, The New School**

It only takes hard work to change the world, and in *Homeboy Came to Orange*, Ernie Thompson offers the honest details that people tend to forget. You have to build bridges, to other groups, to young people, to people you like and don't like, and you must treat everyone as an equal. Thompson didn't just know these things. He lived them and embodied them. He helped people see that what's morally right is politically astute and that the racist and classist power structures you are fighting against want nothing more than for you to fight among yourselves, rather than organize. Organizing, when it's done right, when people really listen to themselves and each other, isn't just about winning a race or a campaign. It is a collective act of love. More than anything, Ernie Thompson shows us how to love.

—**Robert Sullivan, author,** *My American Revolution*

The re-release of Ernie Thompson's book about his rich life as an anti-racism union and community organizer should be read by young (and other) human beings, who have decided to hold church in the streets, courts, state houses, and ballot boxes in the South (and other) parts the U.S. against the white nationalism of the extremists who have hijacked the Republican Party. The story also reminds us why neoliberalism that refuses to fully address systemic racism and the culture of racism is anemic against the forces of racism, greed and militarism.

—**Rev. Dr. William J. Barber II, co-director of the new Poor People's Campaign, architect of the Moral Monday movement, and past president of the North Carolina NAACP**

HOMEBOY
came to orange

Also by Mindy Thompson Fullilove

Urban Alchemy: Restoring Joy in America's Sorted-Out Cities

*Root Shock: How Tearing Up City Neighborhoods Hurts America
and What We Can Do About It*

*Collective Consciousness and Its Discontents:
Institutional Distributed Cognition,
Racial Policy and Public Health in the United States*
(with Rodrick Wallace)

*The House of Joshua:
Meditations on Family and Place*

HOMEBOY
came to orange

A STORY OF PEOPLE'S POWER

Ernest Thompson *and*
Mindy Thompson Fullilove

newvillagePRESS

Published in the United States by New Village Press, New York
hello@newvillagepress.net; www.newvillagepress.net
New Village Press is a public-benefit, not-for-profit publisher.
Distributed by NYU Press
newvillagepress.nyupress.org

Paperback ISBN-13: 978-1-61332-032-7
Publication Date: May 1, 2018
Third Edition

Library of Congress Cataloging-in-Publication Data

Names: Thompson, Ernie (Labor activist) author. | Fullilove, Mindy Thompson, author.
Title: Homeboy came to Orange : a story of people's power / by Ernest Thompson and Mindy Thompson Fullilove.
Description: Third edition. | New York : New Village Press, 2018. | Includes bibliographical references. | Description based on print version record and CIP data provided by publisher; resource not viewed.
Identifiers: LCCN 2018005128 (print) | LCCN 2018007776 (ebook) | ISBN 9781613320341 (epub) | ISBN 9781613320327 (pbk.)
Subjects: LCSH: Fullilove, Mindy Thompson, author. | United Electrical Radio and Machine Workers of America--Biography. | National Negro Labor Council (U.S.)--Biography. | African American political activists--New Jersey--Orange--Biography. | Labor unions--New Jersey--Officials and employees--Biography. | African Americans--New Jersey--Orange--Biography. | Orange (N.J.)--Biography. | Coalitions--New Jersey--Essex County--History. | New Jersey--Race relations--History.
Classification: LCC F144.O6 (ebook) | LCC F144.O6 F85 2018 (print) | DDC 331.88092 [B] --dc23
LC record available at https://lccn.loc.gov/2018005128

Front cover photo: Ernest Thompson at age 19, photographer unknown.
Back cover photos: Ernest Thompson portrait, photographer unknown. Mindy Thompson Fullilove portrait, photographer Ryan Lash.
Interior images: The author is grateful to UE News Photograph Collection, 1933-1998, UE.14.1, Archives & Special Collections, University of Pittsburgh Library System for use of photos on pp. 106, 107, and 108; to Herb Way for photos on pp. 110, 112, 113, and 187; and to Irving Overby for photo on p. 154. All other images are from the author's family archives; forgiveness begged for missing credits.
Front cover design by Pam Shaw
Interior layout by Rich Brown

Dedicated to

Lorraine Thompson Jones

and

Maggie Thompson

Contents

Foreword by Dominic Moulden   xiii

Acknowledgments   xvii

Introduction by Coleman A. Young   xix

In Memoriam by John W. Alexander   xxiii

I. WHO IS YOU?   1

    1   Maryland Boyhood   2

    2   Jersey City   5

    3   UE Organizer   10

    4   Black Labor: In the Union   14

    5   Black Labor: In the NNLC   21

    6   Strong Men, Stronger   27

    7   Repression   34

II. RETREAT TO THE GHETTO   39

    8   Gerrymander in Orange Park   40

    9   The New Day   50

    10   The Campaign Rolls   59

    11   Building Power   70

    12   Into the Central Arena   75

    13   Gerrymander Again   83

    14   Walk In With Ben   88

    15   Home's Economic Policy in Orange   97

PHOTO GALLERY   101

III. THE RIGHT TO LIVE AND WORK   115

  16 Doc Becomes an Educator   116

  17 Twenty Years of Neglect   121

  18 Community Help to Learning   124

  19 More on the Board   127

  20 A Second Chance   132

  21 The Time is Up   137

  22 Walk On With Ben   141

  23 In the Streets   148

IV. HOMEBOY GOES TO NEWARK   157

  24 Job Democracy   158

  25 Redeem the Cities   167

  26 Crusade for Learning   175

V. ON COALITION   179

  27 Pure Coalition at Last   180

  28 Coalition Old and New   190

What We Learned   194

Postscript to the First Edition   202

Postscript to the Second Edition   206

Afterword by Molly Rose Kaufman   209

Endnotes   216

Index   217

Foreword

ERNIE "BIG TRAIN" THOMPSON is a "Homeboy," a person encouraged and enraged by the injustice inflicted on our beautiful people! Our strong and fragile people. Our courageous and weary people fighting daily to not just survive, but to live happy lives. Homeboy Ernie's story of the people of Orange, New Jersey is about changing the system. It is a long train ride, but worth the wait to see the new day coming!

This beautiful second edition of *Homeboy Came to Orange: A Story of People's Power* is right on time, a real story of organizing — not elegant, not glamorous, and not easy. Yet, it is a joyful struggle, full of fun and play, and meaningful relationships with community love at its core. It is the warm and charming story of "Big Train" rolling down the train tracks of life — organizing, building, and trusting in the people's voice.

Over fifty years ago, Big Train organized a community like many places today where we live, work, and play. He confronted the challenges of urban removal and "root shock" — the groundbreaking theory of social disruption coined by Big Train's brilliant and scholarly daughter, Mindy Thompson Fullilove. "Root shock" is when "people who are displaced experience the traumatic stress reaction to the loss of some or all of their emotional ecosystem." Mindy Thompson Fullilove challenges us and society today to prevent root shock by incorporating community voices into a modern-day New Day

Platform. Written by the community and led by Big Train, the 1958 New Day Platform focused on issues crucial to the community: redevelopment and relocation, unemployment, freeway construction and neighborhood disruption, the school system, civil rights, recreation, juvenile delinquency, and representative government. Amazingly, Mindy connected with an organization called Manna Community Development Corporation, in 2003 in Washington, DC. In 2008, Manna CDC was reinvigorated and renamed ONE DC: Organizing Neighborhood Equity DC, where I have organized for over thirty years. ONE DC uses theories about mass and serial displacement to organize long-time and low-income DC residents to resist urban renewal practices that lead to "Negro removal" and gentrification – the final death knell of root shock.

On a very personal note, writing this preface gives me an opportunity to celebrate the Thompson family and their courage and interest in building people's power. The essential importance of "Homeboy" is as a document of the tremendous effort put into organizing ordinary and working-class people. When I say ordinary and working, I mean the precious respect and dignity Big Train shared and embraced with the people. The intentional care and the delicate concern for the voice of the people. Why is voice important? Because up until this very moment, the Black voice is still silenced, ignored, or neglected. The drama and excitement in the daily struggles and wins of the Orange community journey, are tied to the current voice Orange is preparing to gather and lift up. The voices of Orange must be heard, whether is it the voice of the past remembering the New Day Platform or the voice of the present coming from the University of Orange – the brilliant free school which teaches, organizes, and prepares the voices of tomorrow in Orange to create a just city. Orange is under siege by the forces of gentrification and community displacement.

I want to take the liberty to take an excerpt directly from the book, as it captures what we all can be inspired by to move the train of justice forward in our cities with strong, powerful, and brilliant working-class people. It's a favorite part of mine in the first edition of *Homeboy*, the photo of young Mindy with the wonderfully brave Paul Robeson. "Time and again Paul went out of his way to make me feel, 'You're somebody.' He taught me the dignity of the 'least of these.' This has been my guide. The need is to extend this concept so that it is embraced by the Black middle class." Now this is a very mindful and conscious class observation from Big Train, and I am moved by him and Robeson's life story.

Big Train won many organizing victories around school issues, national jobs campaigns, and within the union. However, as all organizers will learn, there are many losses too. You must retreat and come back strong. Two of the best lines that leap off the pages for me are: "Ernie moved to Orange under protest" and "Ernie was considered something of a subversive."

What makes a person an outstanding organizer? The ability to get people to resist and protest, and the ability to build power to subvert an unjust system. Let's give a few big cheers for Big Train! I know most of us organizers want to be known for and connected to such words. For Big Train, these are not just words. This was his life. Justice for Orange – his people-power story – is very much alive today in Washington, DC, where Mindy presented for the first time on January 21, 2005 to our ONE DC members about her book, *Root Shock: How Tearing Up City Neighborhoods Hurts America and What We Can Do About It*. Sounds like the child of Big Train.

What can we do about it?

ONE DC marches to the tune of Ella Jo Baker and her grassroots leadership style. Ms. Baker also captures Big Train's organizing life story when she said: "in order for us as poor and oppressed people to become a part of a society that is meaningful, the system under which we now exist has to be radically changed. This means that we are going to have to learn to think in radical terms. I use the term radical in its original meaning – getting down to understanding the root cause. It means facing a system that does not lend itself to your needs and devising means by which you change that system."

Ten years after Mindy visited us and almost fifty years after Big Train and the Orange community drafted their New Day Platform, the members of ONE DC literally retreated and emerged from the woods of the Wayside Popular Education Center, in Faber, Virginia, with the idea of writing a People's Platform Manifesto. The People's Platform roots are in the voice of the low-income, working-class, Black base of ONE DC in all eight wards of Washington, DC. A People's Platform Coordinating Committee was created to draft the official People's Platform Manifesto which encompasses the right to housing, work, health, government transparency, equitable access to education, prison abolition, safe transportation, restorative justice, as well as the right of return and reclamation for those who have been forced out of their homes by gentrification. The spirit of Ernest "Big Train Homeboy" Thompson is in the words, the people, and the organizing campaigns inspired by the ONE DC People's Platform.

The New Day is coming again and it is in Orange, DC, and many other places on this continent and other global spaces where grassroots leaders and workers are organizing to create just cities and spaces in order to live healthy and happy lives.

—Dominic Moulden,
Washington, DC,
January 2018

Acknowledgments

This book exists because of the dedication of my parents, Ernest and Margaret Thompson, to social justice. They wanted all people to have an equal chance to live, work, and love in our society and around the world. The hard work of my dad was complemented by that of my mom, who maintained our household, ran the mimeograph machine that sat on the kitchen table, translated children's books into Initial Teaching Alphabet (ita), and found camp scholarships for the children in our neighborhood. She was responsible for seeing that the original edition of this book got into print; wresting the manuscript out of my hands, then managing the typesetting, layout, illustration, and printing. She did one other crucial thing. She archived the original illustrations, which made it possible to use them to bring this new edition to life.

The members of Citizens for Representative Government and others in Dad's network of organizations worked with me diligently to tell the story. I spent hours with Dr. John Alexander, Eddie Andrade, Ben Jones, and Mayor Coleman Young among others, learning first-hand about their work. Dr. Alexander contributed the eulogy he delivered at Ernie's memorial service in 1971. Eventually, when the book had been turned down by the mainstream press, they raised the money for printing it. We contracted with Harvard Printing Company in Orange, New Jersey, to do the work. To citizens of Orange and Newark, to the members of UE and the National Negro Labor Council, my undying gratitude for all you have done to fight for a better world. The many artists whose work is included made essential contributions to the work of mobilizing people's power, among them Fred Wright, Charles White, Irving Overby, Herb Way, and Don Miller. I am thrilled that this book holds their art and I offer them my great thanks.

What started as a third printing evolved into a new edition with the help of a new group of supporters. Pam Shaw designed a cover that captured Homeboy, Khemani Gibson helped with the family archives, Aubrey Murdock advised on illustrations, Rich Brown undertook the layout, and Lynne Elizabeth threw the weight of New Village Press behind us. I am grateful to Dominic Moulden of ONE DC for writing a new foreword, and to Molly Rose Kaufman for contributing an afterword.

I was, for many years, embarrassed by my own effort in writing this book. With time, however, I learned that I was wrong; the important fact is that the book exists to tell this important story. I was inspired to re-issue it now because its message is vital in these difficult times of escalating racism, obscene concentration of wealth, and incessant warfare. In particular, I wanted people to have this lesson on the power of coalition as we contemplate 2019 as the 400th anniversary of the first Africans arriving in Jamestown. Dad envisioned this book as a guide to help the powerless build power, to teach them the fundamental lesson of coalition as the essential path forward. I think this book has been patiently waiting for its moment, and its moment is now. My final thanks are to the book, for being here now, when we need it so badly.

—Mindy Thompson Fullilove
February, 2018

Introduction

THE PUBLICATION of this biography of Ernie "Big Train" Thompson is an event of enormous importance – not only for the history of his times, but more importantly as a guide for the future.

"Big Train" was a towering figure among that group of Blacks who saw that World War II was a turning point in the status of racism in the United States, who saw the labor movement as a critical arena in the struggle for liberation, and who understood the decisive importance of coalition.

In 1970, a group of us who were instrumental in creating the National Negro Labor Council celebrated our 20th anniversary by convening to discuss some of the lessons of the preceding twenty years. In honor of "Big Train's" unusual contribution to our efforts, we held the meeting in Newark, where he was then applying coalition tactics to political work in local communities.

Some of the thoughts I expressed then are, I believe, an appropriate introduction to this book.

We had a big discussion prior to our formation of the NNLC on whether we should admit white people. And there were some who said we should call it the National Labor Council, leaving out the word Negro. This is a question that plagues the Black community today, too: How shall we do our thing? Can we make it out there on our own? By ourselves? Or do we need to engage in coalition politics?

Most of us did not have the advantage of higher education, but we could count. We knew what ten meant in relation to ninety. And although we were proud of our prowess as Black men, we decided we would need some help to raise that ten.

We understood in 1951 that coalition meant partnership; it meant a coming together of equals. It did not mean the Black man sitting on Massa's knee, which had been the definition of coalition politics until that time. What I'm trying to say was most classically demonstrated in the speech of our president, Bill Hood, at our founding convention – and that speech was mainly "Big Train's" brainchild – when we said, addressing ourselves to the trade union movement, that we ask for your *cooperation*, but not your *permission*.

But what do *we* do when we get to 51 percent of the population? I was schooled in the game of winner-take-all. But I know that the millennium is not reached when control of, say, a city is gained. Under our system of government, cities, counties, and school districts are creatures of the state. And the state reserves to itself all rights not specifically given to the body involved. So as Black people move to positions of power, we see a national movement toward metropolitan government and county government. That means that even though we successfully win political positions on a local level, the necessity for coalition remains.

In my opinion, if America is to be saved, it will be saved by coalition. The NNLC was drowned in a wave of repression characterized historically as the McCarthy era. We were wiped off the scene. It's my opinion that we are headed now for a period of repression that will make McCarthyism seem like children's games. There, at least, the government operated within the format of the law. But today, the repression is taking on another form: They are arresting, trying, judging, and executing Blacks on our streets. Justice comes out of the muzzle of a police gun.

I don't think this country will ever be the same after the explosions of 1966 and 1967. It has been obvious that we have only two ways to deal with the basic problem which threatens to tear our country apart. We can either go the hard, costly, right way of taking the necessary social steps to remove the causes of the explosion – in other words, take that raisin out of the sun and give it some shade – or we can stand by and watch that raisin swell, and all be inundated in its explosion.

The only way we can repel those who would repress the Black people, in my opinion, is to consolidate our ranks and reach out to our potential allies. In the NNLC, I think we over-estimated the potential support of the trade union movement and under-estimated the necessity of rooting ourselves in the ghetto. I don't think we will make that mistake again. If there is anything that the younger generation – who are now at the switch of the Freedom Train – can learn from our history, it is to not make that same mistake again.

Ernie Thompson's life and work are an enduring guide.

—Coleman A. Young
Detroit, Michigan
January, 1971

In Memoriam

Ernest Thompson died on January 25, 1971.
At his memorial service at Union Baptist Church
in Orange, Dr. John W. Alexander, a longtime friend
and colleague, delivered the main eulogy.

Dear God,

Ernie Thompson just arrived in Heaven a couple of days ago. You may not know he's there yet because it's been a long rough road, and he is tired after battling back from a major stroke, removal of a kidney, a day-long operation on his blood vessels, a serious heart attack, peritonitis, kidney failure, and months on the kidney machine.

But he didn't have time to lay down and be sick. He helped direct one city election from a hospital bed, and he negotiated a quarter-million-dollar agreement within one week after discharge from the hospital, not to mention several lesser accomplishments. He could always talk on the telephone to reach his old friends, union leaders, elected officials, and artists, and corral their resources for such efforts as electing the first Black mayors in Newark and East Orange, and the first Black commissioner in Orange.

I remember when Ernie first came to Orange. He'd been in a tough fight then too. He fought for principle with a major labor union and he fought the red-hunters in the federal government over employment equality for Blacks, women, and all minorities.

The National Negro Labor Council got wiped out, and Ernie was down but not out. He came to Orange to lick his wounds and stew in his own juice.

He quickly recovered when he saw the all-Black Oakwood School had been gerrymandered. He used his many skills learned in labor organizing to breathe life into his ad hoc committee. This first fight in Orange he won with a one-two punch to the Board of Education.

Then he moved into the political arena, where he was the champ. He was schooled in the basics of Hague's Jersey City politics; nobody could match his talents. He put together a campaign and turned it into a fifty-day people's movement that forged Orange's Black community into a political force that now provides the programmatic leadership and is still getting stronger.

He taught us about *Strong Men:*[1]

> *They dragged you from homeland,*
> *They chained you in coffles,*
> *They huddled you spoon-fashion in filthy hatches,*
> *They sold you to give a few gentlemen ease.*
>
> *They broke you in like oxen,*
> *They scourged you,*
> *They branded you,*
> *They made your women breeders,*
>
> *They swelled your numbers with bastards...*
> *They taught you the religion they disgraced.*

You sang:
   Keep a inchin' along
   Lak a po' inch worm...

You sang:
   By and bye
   I'm gonna lay down dis heaby load...

You sang:
   Walk togedder, chillen,
   Dontcha git weary...
         The strong men keep a-comin' on
         The strong men git stronger.

Lord, if you didn't hear that Ernie had arrived, check with St. Peter. Ernie's the one that asked on his arrival, "Where is the ghetto so I can get a taste?" He needed a taste bad. He's been a long time without one. Oh yes, he bummed a cigarette too. I never did get him to quit smoking.

I'm sure St. Peter will remember him because he asked some unheavenly questions about segregation and the school system and your hiring policies. Now, all of us down here know that the Promised Land wouldn't have no mess like that up there. But Home – that's what his friends call him – he always checks things out for himself. He don't take nobody's word for nothin'.

See, God, when he first came to Orange, the Man told him there was no gerrymandering, but Home saw that line through the Park, and he started to fight and Lord, this place ain't been the same since. So Lord, if there's any gerrymandering up there, you got some big trouble coming from Big Train – that's what they called him in the union.

While I been talking, did you check with St. Peter about that new Black arrival that was looking into what you pay the female angels? Well, I'm here to tell you that Home spent most of his life fighting for equal pay for equal work. He took on the industrial giants and won that round. He wasn't no fancy dancer and he had only one trick – like the cat, up the programmatic tree.

Lord, so there won't be no trouble, check out the salary scales, and the policies on job opportunity, and hiring and firing, and promotion, and seniority. And, by the way, if you got anybody hustling piecework, Home is an expert in that field. When he gets you into negotiations, remember I told you to watch your pennies, 'cause Ernie will haggle a week for a mill after he does a time study and finds out where they are getting cheated.

   Since you're the Boss of the Land of Milk and Honey, I guess the working conditions are pretty good, but you wouldn't have any sweetheart contracts, would you? Home is a real bloodhound when it comes to sniffing out a stinking deal, and I know you don't want any union trouble.

   What did you say? No heavenly unions? Oh, oh, I got news for you. I'm giving odds down here that there'll be an angel union real soon. So you and St. Peter better set up your negotiating team, 'cause Home lived through a year of the head-busting tactics of Jersey City police to break his first long successful strike. You better check how sharp his mind is by taking him on in some bridge or cooncan or poker before you get into negotiations so his appearance doesn't mislead you. And by the way, if he falls asleep on you, don't say nothing you don't want him to know. He's the only man I've ever seen that could still hear everything even while he was catching a quick nap.

Lord, in a few days Home will be well rested, and you'll find him with the boys in the ghetto, and I can assure you he'll be talking about representation and coalition. You see, in

Orange, he taught us Blacks about our history and our culture. He taught us self-pride and self-respect. He taught us that a combination of middle-class Blacks, with their education, and the Black masses, working hand in hand, could win. But he had to teach us *Strong Men* so we could see how our minds had been screwed up.

> *They point with pride to the roads you built for them,*
> *They ride in comfort over the rails you laid for them.*
> *They put hammers in your hand*
> *And said – Drive so much before sundown.*

> *You sang:*
> > *Ain't no hammah*
> > *In dis lan',*
> > *Strikes lak mine, bebby,*
> > *Strikes lak mine.*

> *They cooped you in their kitchens,*
> *They penned you in their factories,*
> *They gave you the jobs that they were too good for,*
> *They tried to guarantee happiness to themselves*
> *By shunting dirt and misery to you.*

> *You sang:*
> > *Me an' muh baby gonna shine, shine*
> > *Me an' muh baby gonna shine.*
> > > The strong men keep a-comin' on
> > > The strong men git stronger...

Lord, among all them other lessons, Home taught us Blacks to fight for equality with his foot. He applied his pointy-toed shoe to the seat of our pants every time we made a mistake. When we learned how to stand up like real men, he then taught us tactics. And finally he taught us coalition – how the minority can seek allies in the white community and give leadership to the resulting alliance.

Some of the cats down here are secretly relieved that Home is off their backs so they can go back to masturbating in the ghetto. They wasn't really happy when Home put the whip on them and made them fight the Man in the main arena. And you should have seen the way some of them would try to hide when Ernie started twirling the blackjack on Mr. Charlie. So some of these cats are already planning on going back to the old vest-pocket operation and selling out their brothers and sisters, like Sterling Brown said:

> *They bought off some of your leaders*
> *You stumbled, as blind men will…*
> *They coaxed you, unwontedly soft-voiced…*
> *You followed a way.*
> *Then laughed as usual.*
> *They heard the laugh and wondered;*
> *Uncomfortable;*
> *Unadmitting a deeper terror…*
>> The strong men keep a-comin' on
>> Gittin' stronger…

So, thanks to Ernie, the Black community in Orange, East Orange, Montclair, and Newark is now a better example of what Sterling Brown was talking about when he wrote *Strong Men*.

Now that Home is up there with you where the streets are paved with gold, I know he was glad to see decent housing for Black people. When he was down here, he wasn't much on Urban Renewal, which he called *People Removal*, but he was a real bug on rehab. You know he breathed life into Tri-City.

The Governor of New Jersey just yesterday opened the second part of Ernie's brainchild, Amity II. When private developers took over, Ernie also negotiated $250,000 for community health, education, and recreation programs in Amity Village. So if you have any substandard housing, start rehab right away because me and some of his friends down here are not anxious for Ernie to expand *Tri*-Cities into *Four*-Cities!

Dear God, you are the Master of all and I know you want the best for all the little children. Home is the champion of "the least of these." I'm sure your educational system is something to behold, but I hope your curriculum is relevant to the Heaven of Work, and that it includes Black History as an integral part of human history, and not stuck off to the side like a bump on a log like it's done too often down here. And from the beautiful voices of the angel choirs, I know music and cultural arts are included. For your information, God, Home has researched education from Pavlov's experiments in teaching dogs to the computerized teaching typewriter. He met with educational experts from Harvard, Stevens Institute of Technology, and many other universities. It was always with amazement and respect that I watched this unlettered Black man invade the ivory towers and match his wits against the best-trained minds in this country. Lord, I don't know what your residency requirements are, but I think you ought to consider him for your next appointment to your heavenly Board of Education.

Home was my close friend, Lord, and a master of language arts. He had what we called the *Big Ear*. When Home spoke, he said things so clearly that everyone knew exactly what he meant. And when Home listened, he heard exactly what the other guy meant, even though some of us had missed the hidden meaning. When Home gave you his word, it was his bond. In all the years I knew him, his integrity was unquestioned even by his enemies, of which he had many.

He wasn't never scared of a fight, either. When he took on a fight, he studied the situation thoroughly; he never came off the wall. If he wasn't ready, his only answer was "Huh?" He always warned us that Johnny-come-lately ain't supposed to whip the champ, but he showed us that superior preparation can overcome superior forces.

I'm saying all this to kind of warn you. They say that a word to the wise is sufficient, and I know you know all. Well, Home spent his life straightening out this place and making it better for us and our children. Now he is in Heaven to rest and sit at your right hand. But if the place ain't straight, Lord, Home will be stewing in his own juice again like when he first came to Orange, and before long, he'll be getting registered and checking on the date of the next election.

Now, I don't know how long you been Head Man up there, but from what I hear it's been a long time. I know Home doesn't intend to run for the high office himself, but maybe St. Peter or one of the others would make a good democratic candidate, and I know from personal experience Home will be the campaign manager. In fact, he may have already convinced St. Peter like he convinced me to run in Orange. My life has not been the same since, and I have Home to thank for making me a man I would not have been, had it not been for him and his teachings.

Home spent a lifetime working with us poor mortals. I think it would be a good idea if you made him Chief of the Department of Creativity. He could make man over in your image without a mind diseased with racism. Ernie almost got the job done down here with only your moral support. The two of you as a coalition could make man into a real human being capable of real brotherly love.

xxx

XXXI

What, from the slums
Where they have hemmed you,
What, from the tiny huts
They could not keep from you –
What reaches them
Making them ill at ease, fearful?
Today they shout prohibition at you
"Thou shalt not this"
"Thou shalt not that"
"Reserved for whites only"
You laugh.

One thing they cannot prohibit –

    The strong men... coming on

    The strong men gittin' stronger.

    Strong men...

    Stronger...

I. WHO IS YOU?

Ernie Thompson was speaking on the mike at the corner
of Parrow and Central Place, heart of the Orange ghetto –
the Corner of Good Hope where campaigns began
and ended.

He saw a man come out of a bar and head directly towards
him. He kept speaking and the man kept coming. When
he reached Ernie, he shouted, "Who is you?"

Ernie was thrown off balance for a few seconds but finally
he said, "I'm Homeboy. I'm with you. Is you with me?"

The man smiled and said, "Carry on, Homeboy, I'm
with you."

1   Maryland Boyhood

It is no easy thing for a young Black man or a young Black woman to live in the South today... They are in the midst of a legal caste and customary insults; they are in continuous danger of mob violence; they are mistreated by the officers of the law and they have no hearing before the courts and the churches and public opinion commensurate with the attention which they ought to receive...

To rescue this land... calls for the Great Sacrifice; this is the thing that you are called upon to do because it is the right thing to do. Because you are embarked upon a great and holy crusade, the emancipation of mankind, black and white...[2]

W.E.B. Du Bois

ERNIE THOMPSON GREW UP on his grandfather's farm on the Eastern Shore of Maryland. As a young boy, he raised sweet potatoes to sell. One day, a pig invaded the field and destroyed his young plants.

His father, Joshua, helped him catch the pig. "Son, we'll keep the animal and feed him until his owner comes to claim him. When he pays us for his keep, we'll buy you some new plants."

Two days later a white farmer who lived down the road came for his pig.

"We have your pig and you can take him just as soon as you pay me for his keep," Josh Thompson said.

"Ain't gonna pay you nothing," the white man replied.

He and his field hand started to load the pig into the buggy. Ernie ran into the house and came out with his father's loaded shotgun. He aimed it at the farmer, and shouted, "You can't take that pig until you pay!"

"Get that gun away from him, Josh," yelled the farmer.

Josh turned to Ernie. "Come on, boy, give me the gun. I'll take care of it."

Ernie obeyed. Josh lowered the hammer. The field hand loaded the pig. The white farmer paid nothing and drove away.

Ernie watched him go. For a moment he'd seemed to have power in his hands, but it had been taken away. As he grew older, he resolved to get some real power.

Life was rough for the Black farmers on Chesapeake Bay. They struggled to eke out a living from tiny parcels of land. For the Thompsons it was not enough. They frequently had to leave home to earn money, Josh cooking on ships and Jennie for wealthy families in Baltimore.

Josh and Jennie were determined that their five children would have a better life. Lorraine, Olin, Ernest, Sarah, and Robert lived by Josh Thompson's strict rule: "When you leave school, you leave here." Other families took their big boys and girls out of school; Josh insisted that his children continue. Ernie, at eleven and twelve, wanted to hire out so that he could have money in his pockets and rent a buggy for driving on Sundays. Instead he stayed in school all winter, five or six months more than his friends.

"Why do *I* have to go to school?" he protested.

"You have to go to school so you can *be* something," his father replied. "You got to learn to read and write just like the white man's boy, and then there's nothing they can hide from you. You can find it out for yourself."

His schooling gave Ernie some advantages. When the big boys came into school from the fields, they were behind in reading. Ernie tutored them, which gave him a chance to be with them.

He read the Bible to Philip Henry Thompson, his grandfather. In return, the older man told him stories of his days under slavery. One story Ernie always remembered was of a slave who worked in the Big House and ingratiated himself by carrying tales on the other slaves. They finally caught him at it and chopped off his big toe. It was impossible for Ernie to forget the moral of the story; he saw the old man his grandfather had told him about go limping by every day.

He was also able to read of the history and culture of his people. Though books were scarce, he read and re-read *Uncle Tom's Cabin*, *The Negro Soldier in World War I* [originally titled *Sidelights on Negro Soldiers*], and the poetry of Paul Laurence Dunbar and Phyllis Wheatley.

Ernie hated the grinding poverty of the countryside and longed to get away. Finally, after promising his mother that he would finish school, he moved North to live with an aunt in Jersey City, New Jersey.

2   Jersey City

It was in Jersey City that the direction of Ernie's life work began to emerge. His political education started in the schoolyards. His aunt's home was in the ghetto. Between it and his school lay hostile territory: an Irish neighborhood where the boys resented his attendance at their overwhelmingly white school. He had to fight his way morning and night. His "down home" fighting style helped, but his first line of defense was that he organized his friends. Together they fought the whites to get to school.

Later, Ernie went to an evening high school so that he could work while continuing his education. He found a job in a bowling alley. The pay was low and the hours were long, so he organized all the pinsetters to ask for a raise. They went in a body to see the boss. Ernie was the spokesman: He expressed their dissatisfaction and their demand for better wages.

The boss said, "Now I hear what *you* say, Ernie, and I'm surprised." Turning to the others, he asked, "Do you boys really think those things?" As he looked from one to the other, they all retreated.

"Well, Ernie," said the boss, "since you don't like it here, you don't have to work here anymore."

Ernie found himself alone and out of work.

At sixteen, he got his first factory job. During slow times, he worked as a sandhog or coal miner. While he was working on the construction of the Holland Tunnel, he got the bends and had to be hospitalized. During his stay in the hospital, news came that his whole crew had been killed. He jumped out of bed and ran all the way home, swearing never to work as a sandhog again.

When Ernie could, he got steady work in the American Radiator plant in Bayonne. He made cores in the foundry. Like most other factories in the 1930s, it was hot and dirty, and the employees put in long hours for low pay. The company did all it could to ensure the powerlessness of the workers. It organized the work force into racial and national groups: Anglo-Saxons in mechanical and warehouse jobs, Italians in first test, Poles in core and second test, and Blacks and Hispanics in the foundry.

The employers profited from this racist system. The existence of conflicting groups of workers denied to all workers the power created by unity. The American Federation of Labor (AFL), which dominated the labor movement then, played into the hands of the employers. It espoused craft unionism, opposed militant struggle, and refused to take a decisive stand on organizing Black workers on a non-discriminatory basis.

Dramatic change came with the Great Depression. The dire need of the workers forced them to unite regardless of job classification, race, sex, or creed. The workers finally had the strength to win their basic demands – job security and a wage base. They had to put aside their differences, and they started the move for industrial unionism, the very nature of which was opposed to the racial divisions common in the AFL. Without racial equality, the mass industrial unions could not have been built.

Ernie and his fellow workers in American Radiator began organizing in 1934, starting with the Blacks in the foundry. It was easy enough from there to join with the Spanish-speaking workers. Though a minority in the plant, the Blacks and Hispanics, tightly organized and militant, earned the respect of the whites in the other departments, which laid a basis for unity.

Ernie learned then that Black leadership was acceptable to whites if there was common ground. This was confirmed inadvertently when he overheard a conversation in the lunchroom. Some whites from another plant were sitting at a nearby table with white workers from American Radiator. "I see you got niggers for shop stewards here," sneered one of the outsiders.

"Hell, yeah," said the Radiator worker. "Niggers are willing to fight."

Unity based on strength was essential. But the workers were inexperienced and made a tactical error by striking while there was a warehouse full of unsold goods. The strike lasted nine long months through a bitterly cold and hungry winter. Ernie walked the snowy picket lines with cardboard filling the holes in his shoes. His mother-in-law, with whom he and his family were living, was against the union. As the strike wore on, she put him out in the street, saying it was enough that she was supporting his wife Emma and their child. Somehow, Ernie managed to live through the strike. His daily diet was a bag of peanuts and a quart of milk. ·

While the strike was in process, the Radiator workers were signed by the AFL Foundry Workers Union, but were later abandoned by that union when strikebreakers began entering the plant. Other unions crossed the picket lines to haul goods. A wire fence was built to keep the strikers out.

The pressure eventually became too great, and the strike was lost. But the workers had gained a deeper sense of unity and had learned to put aside their differences to struggle for wages, seniority, a written contract, and grievance machinery.

Out of the strike an independent union was born. It was weak, but Ernie fought to make the most of the strength it did have. He stood firm in grievance procedures, such as they were, and worked tirelessly to build unity. When he was elected president in 1940, he led a struggle to take the shop into an international union, the United Electrical, Radio and Machine Workers of America (UE), then one of the leading militant unions of the newly born Congress of Industrial Organizations (CIO).

Back home in the ghetto, though, the union's power did not suffice. It could not stop children from having to go to inferior schools, or landlords' neglect, or cops' abuse of innocent persons. Unions themselves, encouraged by the Wagner Act, had been born of political power. Ernie had long believed that the workers needed political power to maintain the union as well as to better other areas of their lives. When he could, he organized political clubs and involved union members in local politics – something he had been doing since he was fourteen and started his first Democratic club in Jersey City.

Ernie lived in Jersey City during the heyday of one of the most awesome political machines this nation has seen, that of Frank Hague, "the Boss." Hague controlled Jersey City, Hudson County, and much of New Jersey, rising to power in the 1910s and holding sway for most of the next three decades.

In 1935, Ernie and a small community political group asked Hague to put their candidate on the Democratic slate for State Assembly. Hague refused.

"To hell with that," said Ernie, "we'll go after it," and he ran his man as a Democrat against the regular ticket.

But Blacks in Jersey City were only 2 percent of the population. Without the support of the Democratic machine, it was impossible to make a significant showing. It was a lesson Ernie never forgot.

In 1943, Ernie left the shop, at the request of the union, to manage the campaign of a labor candidate in Bayonne. That candidate, running alone, got over 10 percent of the vote against bracketed candidates who pooled their money and organization. By then Ernie had learned organizational techniques as well as how to relate organization in the shops to political organization.

After this showing, he was able to talk turkey with Hague about programs labor wanted. Labor immediately got a candidate – John Grogan, later mayor of Hoboken – on Hague's Assembly ticket. Labor had a leg up on some political power, and in the Boss's stronghold at that.

3   UE Organizer

FOLLOWING THIS 1943 election campaign, Ernie was asked to leave the shop to become the first Black organizer for his union. Some of the white leaders of the union, however, wanted to confine his work to organizing Black workers.

One of those leaders showed up at a local meeting and asked for volunteers to leaflet a nearby unorganized plant. He was quick to tell Ernie, "You can't come. It's mostly white workers and you can't organize white workers."

Ernie replied, "Well, I'm part of this union, and I don't accept that view. We built this union on the basis of no discrimination. We don't come together because we're Black and white; we come together because we're workers. You try to keep me from white workers because I'm Black, you'll undermine that unity."

He and Bill Jackson, a Black man and his staunchest friend in the Radiator plant, took some of the leaflets and made the gates the next morning. No one else from the union showed up. Not a single worker refused a leaflet. The plant was not far from where Bill and Ernie lived, so they took over the organizing by getting up early to be at the plant gates to talk to the workers. No white workers objected. The union leader continued his effort to confine Ernie's work to Black workers, but proof in the field had destroyed his argument.

Ernie's understanding of Hague and life in Jersey City was of help in his union work. During a tough Westinghouse strike, Ernie sent out a rumor that the union was going to break an injunction and set up a massive picket line. The next morning, hundreds of mounted police, swinging their billy clubs, descended on three women calmly patrolling the plant gates. It was such an embarrassment to Hague that thereafter he let the union picket at will.

Ernie proved himself to be a capable organizer and leader. He worked hard, and his dedication and leadership were accepted by Black and white workers. During the war years, his union formed an amalgamated local in Hudson County, and Ernie was elected business manager several times, despite the white majority in the local.

Perhaps of even more significance in proving the acceptability of Black leadership to white workers was his role in the Hudson County Industrial Union Council, CIO. He was first a vice-president and subsequently the executive secretary of the council, which included 50,000 shipyard workers alone. Ernie's job was to build political power for the workers. During his term in office, labor ran a number of candidates on a city, county, or state basis, through the Political Action Committee (CIO-PAC). The council was foremost in support of Franklin D. Roosevelt and his policies.

When Roosevelt ran for his fourth term in 1944 – the closest of his elections – the Hudson County CIO-PAC helped return a substantial majority in its area. Tens of thousands of workers from shops, shipyards, and plants showed up for a giant rally in Journal Square. Labor and political leaders spoke on FDR's program, which was basically the CIO program: victory in the war, full employment afterwards, and a better America.

In the post-war period, the bankers and industrialists were frightened by the domestic impact of the war, the growing strength of the unions, and the rising demands of the colonial world for the right to self-determination. They used racism and the fear of communism to divide the people and push them back.

UE was one of the number of front-line progressive unions that had policies of equality of Black and white, and male and female. It was opposed to colonialism and stood for coexistence in a world of peace. It split with the CIO in 1946 because of furious red-baiting against it, a situation instigated after the war by reactionary forces determined to beat back labor and other progressives who had moved forward under the New Deal. Some forces in the labor movement, including at the time the leadership of the CIO, were manipulated to play an important role in this tactic.

The CIO formed a rival union, the International Union of Electrical, Radio and Machine Workers of America (IUE), to raid UE. Ernie was called upon to help defend UE and did some of his best organizing work. Day and night, he traveled from shop to shop showing the workers how UE's policies had bettered their lives. Blacks were particularly aware of the dangers of disunity, and that made Ernie's role in the struggle for the union even more critical.

One of the particularly tough struggles took place in Baltimore in 1950, where racial as well as political disunity was used in an attempt to destroy the union. General Electric initiated speedup and simultaneous wage cuts at its Locke Insulator plant. It began the program in the kiln department – all Black – where temperatures reached 180 degrees. Manpower was reduced by one-third and wages were cut as much as 50 percent. The tactic was to split union opposition by dividing the workers across racial lines. There was no way the union could win except by hitting the racism, yet many of the union leaders were afraid to take the issue head-on. Ernie held a hard line in those situations: racism would not be allowed to divide the workers.

At first the white workers stood by the Blacks. But the company was not yet through. As Ernie described it, "After a few days of the strike, lo and behold there appeared in the *Baltimore Sun* an ad saying, 'Negro workers wanted for Locke Insulator.' In all the years, this had never happened before.

"The over 50,000 unemployed Black workers in Baltimore woke up and were sure manna was raining from heaven. Thousands rushed down to the banks of the Patapsco, only to be told there was a strike on and they were being asked to break it. But the scheme failed. The unemployed workers saw the dirty trick that was being played on them and stood united with their Black fellow workers who were on strike... The company was forced to retreat."

4 Black Labor: In the Union

THE GREAT DEPRESSION, followed shortly by World War II, was a turning point for Black Americans. Ernie, who had studied the history of slavery and the struggle for the liberation of the Black people, recognized the extraordinary changes that had been triggered by these events.

The promise of freedom that had earlier emerged from the Civil War and the Emancipation Proclamation proved to be hollow. As the United States became an industrial nation, Black people were kept out of the mainstream of its development. The building of the CIO represented a great democratic advance because it essentially rejected the racist policies that had previously dominated the labor movement.

The CIO was barely five years old when the nation found itself in World War II. The American industrial machine now turned to Black America, as it did to women, as a matter of necessity. Every worker was needed. The result was that the progress toward non-discrimination which had been made with the growth of industrial trade unionism was greatly magnified. This beachhead in industry was supported by President Franklin D. Roosevelt who created the first Fair Employment Practices Committee (FEPC) in 1941 by Executive Order 8802, which banned discrimination in the defense industry. Established after mass pressure from the Black community, the FEPC offered a way of fighting job discrimination.

Simultaneously, a whole new situation was brewing for Black workers. Mechanization began on the countryside. No longer did the crops require the labor of many hands, and the laborers were thrown off the land. The 1940s saw a second great migration of Black people, their belongings strapped on their backs, making the weary trek North.

The end of the war brought immediate erosion of the wartime gains. With the end of war production, Black workers, who had been "last hired," were the lowest in seniority and the "first fired." Conditions in the Black community worsened.

On a world scale, the foundations of imperialism were shaken as first Eastern Europe and then China became socialist, and the peoples of Africa and Asia began to demand independence. The response of the U.S. government to this progress was reaction at home and war abroad. Some of the earliest victims of the McCarthy-anticommunist terror were militant CIO unions like UE.

Accompanying a vicious attack on civil liberties was an attack on civil rights. Black people were being killed and framed all over the country. The late 1940s and early 1950s was the time of the harassment and imprisonment of Rosa Lee Ingram, Willie McGee, the Martinsville Seven, the Trenton Six, and others whose main crime was being Black. The Black community had little political representation and throughout much of the South was denied the right to vote.

To Ernie and other Black trade union leaders, it became clear that a new kind of struggle was needed, based on unity of Black workers in strong coalition with white brothers and sisters.

As part of the struggle to strengthen coalition within his union, Ernie felt it was necessary to have a caucus in which Black workers met separately to discuss their problems and formulate policy. UE's Black caucus was one of the first in the country. Through a combination of the union's commitment to coalition and their experiences in their own Black caucus, the Black leadership of UE was at the forefront of the National Trade Union Conference for Negro Rights, held in 1950.

country. Through a combination of the union's commitment to coalition and their experiences in their own Black caucus, the Black leadership of UE was at the forefront of the National Trade Union Conference for Negro Rights, held in 1950.

Paul Robeson, the militant Black singer and actor, inspired the 900 trade unionists who gathered in Chicago. Speaking from his deep faith in the working class and his devotion to liberation, he told them:

> The Negro trade unionists must increasingly exert their influence in every aspect of the life of the Negro community... You are called upon to provide the spirit, the determination, the organizational skill, the firm steel of unyielding militancy to the age-old strivings of the Negro people for equality and freedom... And to the white trade unionists present – a special challenge. You must fight in the ranks of labor for the full equality of your Negro brothers and sisters...[3]

That conference projected two main goals –

1. that every union establish a Fair Employment Practices Committee, with full-time staff, to struggle for democracy in the unions and the shops; and
2. that a national organization of Black workers be built to fight for economic equality.

UE adopted the complete resolution for a Fair Practices Committee and began to look for a person to fill the position of secretary of the committee. With the consent of the leading Black forces in UE, Ernie was promoted to the job.

The Black caucus continued to develop policy for the committee. They realized that their primary need was for allies.

Blacks were only a small minority in the union. If the program was to be a success, they would need others to fight for it with them. They found their most natural ally in women, another group that was oppressed by the shop and not fully free in the union. The electrical industry had many women workers who had traditionally faced super-exploitation in pay and working conditions. The resulting coalition formed a powerful fighting force.

The coalition of women and Blacks developed many progressive policies and outlooks. They worked in two areas: promoting non-whites and women into leadership positions and developing training programs to prepare workers to advance to higher paying jobs.

The committee was successful in broadening representation and bringing minorities into leadership. At one point, UE had three Blacks and two women on its national executive board of approximately twenty-five, an achievement unequalled by any other union in the country at that time. Most workers affected by discrimination had the feeling that if they were represented on the top executive body – where policy was carried out after being adopted at conventions – their situation would be better. Regardless of whether this was completely true, the committee's success on the leadership level was looked upon with great favor by these workers.

The Fair Practices Committee accomplished a number of "firsts" in developing the training programs it conducted around the country. Many workers were entitled on the basis of seniority to bid for higher jobs. But if they could not read a micrometer or elementary blueprints, they knew in advance they could not succeed and were afraid to "bump" into more skilled jobs. The committee's programs prepared them to move up. Arrangements were made with craftsmen to track the specialization and with boards of education to run special programs of varying duration, including instruction in related math. The whole training outlook was later adopted in the Gateway to the South campaign of the National Negro Labor Council.

One of Ernie's stories of this period illustrates the tightness of the coalition formed between the Black workers and the women in UE.

In the UE shops in the Pennsylvania mountains, the Fair Practices Committee had done a great deal of work to advance the position of women. The women decided to hold a conference to discuss their problems and evaluate solutions. They asked Ernie to come and address their meeting, which he was happy to do. About the time he was supposed to go, a rumor filtered into the national office that "if Thompson comes, we're gonna hang him." A story was going around that he had eyes for one of the white women in Pennsylvania. The women knew this story wasn't true; they also knew who was spreading it. They called Ernie and said, "You come on out here. We'll protect you."

"Well," he said, putting on his hat, "I'm going even if I don't come back."

Ernie arrived at the airport in Pennsylvania and found several cars full of women there to meet him. They took him to a hotel and stood guard outside his room.

During the conference, there was a dance. As he talked with some of the women, one of the organizers came up to him and said, "We want you to dance, and we have your partners all lined up."

"Oh, no," Ernie protested, "I don't care to dance."

"We want you to dance," they insisted. He danced.

The conference was a success. Afterwards, the women drove

him back to the airport and put him on the plane. He made it home safely.

The minority and women workers knew they could count on UE; UE could also count on them. In 1954, Eastern Metal in UE District 4 had about 100 workers. Within six months, it expanded to 500; 400 of them brought in from a CIO shop. That union, Textile Workers, made plans to raid UE.

Frances Gulotta, a UE leader, told the 1955 convention, "Picture yourself in a situation with a hundred people to start and 400 more coming in from a CIO shop. We were in trouble."[4]

They didn't give up. They called a meeting "For Women Only." Despite dire predictions of the male leaders of the union that the women wouldn't come, over a hundred showed up.

"We explained the UE program for women," Gulotta told them, "the annual conference and the fight we have been putting up over the years. The women were really surprised... As a result of our program for women's rights we were able to get many of the women formerly campaigning for CIO to campaign for us."

The women saved the shop for UE. After winning the election, UE in negotiations took on the problem of the women's differential in pay for the same work men did. In the first round, they managed to eliminate three cents of the five-cent differential.

5   Black Labor: In the NNLC

THE 1950 TRADE UNION Convention laid the foundation for the creation of the National Negro Labor Council (NNLC). The idea of uniting the Black working class was not new. It was originally expressed by an organization called the American Negro Labor Congress, founded in Chicago in November 1925. In 1930, the Congress merged with the League of Struggle for Negro Rights, and in time disappeared. During World War II, the Negro Labor Victory Committee played a major role in pressing for jobs for Blacks.

But the NNLC came at a time when Black unionists had a stronger base in organized labor and a high conception of how to use their power. They were joined by some whites who were dedicated to standing with their Black brothers and sisters.

Bill Hood was the president of NNLC. Formerly from Georgia, Hood had come into leadership of the United Auto Workers (UAW) from the foundry of the Ford River Rouge plant, which had been key to building the union and had a tradition of militant struggle. He was an outspoken union leader who had defended the Smith Act victims, Communist party leaders jailed for their beliefs. He brought to the council a high ideal of direction for Black labor, along with the power to back it.

Coleman Young, known as "Big Red," a quick-thinking speaker and able organizer, was the executive secretary. From

Tuscaloosa, Alabama, he had lived in Detroit most of his life. During World War II, he was an officer in the Army Air Corps, a member of the celebrated Tuskegee Airmen. He spent time in the stockade for trying to get a cup of coffee at an all-white officers' club. After the war, he worked for the post office but quit when "they wouldn't give me time off to work for the union." He organized for the Wayne County CIO and the Progressive Party and brought this organizational experience to the council.

Vicki Garvin, vice-president of the Distributive, Processing and Office Workers of America, was one of NNLC's vice-presidents. She had come to the labor movement from Smith College, but it was in the unions that she had her real education.

Maurice Travis, white executive secretary of the Mine, Mill and Smelter Workers, a union which carried on militant struggles for the rights of miners throughout the South, was another NNLC vice-president. Travis had lost an eye in a shoot-out in Alabama where he defended the union against the Ku Klux Klan.

Ernie, called "Big Train" because he could deliver the goods in negotiations, became director of organization. His experience as a shop worker, the first Black organizer for UE, and later secretary of its Fair Practices Committee, gave him a rich background. He was the motor of the NNLC train; he drafted the keynote address of the founding convention and was a leading planner of the strategy of the organization.

The opening day of the founding convention of the NNLC, October 27, 1951, was a memorable event. It was held in Cincinnati, chosen because it had been one of the main stations of the Underground Railroad by which slaves had escaped to the North. Despite its noble history, it was then a Jim Crow city.

Big Train Thompson rose on the podium that Saturday

afternoon to tell the delegates: "We say something new is happening. It gets in your bones; it's on the breezes; it's everywhere. What is it? It's a new wind of freedom blowing from the Seven Seas and touching the hearts of men and women... This new wind has brought on the scene a new Negro, the sons and daughters of labor. They have come with one song in their hearts – *the song of freedom*."[5]

He then recited:

> *Out of the darkness and out of the night*
> *The Black man crawls to the dawn of light,*
> *Beaten by lashes and bound by chains,*
> *Searching, seeking for the Freedom Train.*

"Jolting Joe" Johnson, a West Coast dockworker, leaped up, shouting, "Great God Almighty," and Bill Hood, seated behind Ernie, whispered, "Get me ready, daddy, get me ready!"

Thompson continued:

> *They bought off some of your leaders*
> *You stumbled, as blind men will...*
> *They coaxed you, unwontedly soft-voiced...*
> *You followed a way.*
> *Then laughed as usual.*
>
> *They heard the laugh and wondered;*
> *Uncomfortable;*
> *Unadmitting a deeper terror...*
>> The strong men keep a-comin' on
>> Gittin' stronger...

He presented Hood as a symbol of the new Negro, saying, "Hood speaks for us."

Hood's speech represented months of collective effort and thinking. It set forth the political and programmatic outlook for the council. More importantly, it set forth a vision of the new role for Black labor in the freedom movement:[6]

> No meeting held anywhere in America at this mid-century point in world history can be more important nor hold more promise for the bright future toward which humanity strives than this convention of our great National Negro Labor Council. For here we have gathered this basic force of human progress: the Black sons and daughters of labor and our democratic white brothers and sisters whose increasing concern for democracy, equality, and peace is America's bright hope for tomorrow.

> The Negro Labor Council is our symbol, the medium of expression of our aims and aspirations. It is the expression of our desire and determination to bring to bear our full weight to help win first class citizenship for every Black man, woman and child in America. We say that these are legitimate aims. We say that these aspirations burn fiercely in the breast of the Negro in America. And we further say that millions of white workers echo our demands for freedom. These white workers recognize in the struggle for Negro rights, the prerequisites of their own aspirations for a full life and a guarantee that the rising tide of fascism will not engulf America.

Hood emphasized that the program was to build an organization of Black workers, men and women, united with white workers willing to accept and support their program. The organization was not to compete with existing organizations of the Black people but rather to be a movement of a new type, a movement that could "chart the course ahead to help the whole Negro people and their sincere allies." The organization would bring together the strength of the Black workers to lead the freedom struggle "to the end that you will have economic, political, and social equality, so that you may enjoy the great and good things of our land."

Hopes and fears were expressed in the speech, as well as one absolute demand: "We wish to say further that the day has ended when white trade union leaders or white leaders in any organization may presume to tell Negroes on what basis they shall come together to fight for their rights. Three hundred years has been enough of that. We Black people in America ask for your *cooperation* – but we do not ask for your *permission*!"

There were cries of, "Go, man, go," "Amen, brother," "Now you're talking." Delegates stomped their feet, they clapped, they cheered.

Hood's speech presented a revolutionary new idea. The Black workers proclaimed that *they* would now be the policy makers in their liberation struggle. "Go back to the white community," they told the white workers, "and organize there. That's where your job lies."

This separation of tasks was for the sake of unity. They called for it so that Black and white workers, each having their own organizational base, might come together on the basis of complete democracy and struggle together on matters of common concern.

To many delegates, the high point of the convention came with the appearance of their beloved Paul Robeson, who spoke and sang.

The convention rocked Cincinnati. Jim Crow went underground as 1,100 Black and white workers walked the streets in unity and strength.

A powerful new movement to disrupt the traditions of racism had been launched. Ernie, as organizational director of the NNLC, was at its center.

6   Strong Men, Stronger

THE FIRST NATIONAL JOBS CAMPAIGN of the National Negro Labor Council was a drive to win sales clerk and clerical positions for Black women in the giant Sears-Roebuck department store chain. At that time, Sears followed an ironclad policy of refusing to hire Blacks above the position of janitor. Following an early breakthrough in San Francisco, local councils across the nation joined the fight and mounted picket lines in cities such as Newark, Philadelphia, Cleveland, and Detroit. By the end of 1953, practically all Sears outlets in the North had capitulated except for the Chicago stores. There it took months of picketing and a boycott by the NNLC and other organizations before Sears surrendered.

The fight for jobs in the airlines was also launched at the founding convention. Early in 1952, NNLC exposed the Jim Crow job practices of the airlines in a letter addressed to the then-newly created Committee on Government Contracts, headed by Vice-President Nixon. NNLC requested that the committee accept jurisdiction over the employment policies of the airlines and issue a directive requiring them to come into immediate compliance with fair employment standards required of all firms holding contracts with the U.S. government. The climax of the NNLC airlines campaign came in November 1952. At the second annual convention in Cleveland, some 1,500 delegates staged a mass picket line and jobs demonstration

in the airlines ticket center in downtown Cleveland. This demonstration put the national spotlight on the undemocratic employment practices of the airlines. Many other organizations later added their voices to that of the NNLC, and eventually discrimination in the airlines was broken.

The railroad industry was selected as the key to the jobs fight waged by NNLC for several reasons: first, it was largely Black working people, together with Irish immigrants, who performed the tremendous job of constructing the vast network of rails that united this country. Not by accident was the hero of the rails the mighty John Henry, a Black man.

Second, the railroads led the way in brutal exploitation of Black workers as a source of cheap labor. Until World War I, it was usual for the railroads in the Southern and border states to use Negro firemen, brakemen, and trainmen on 25 percent to 90 percent of their runs. Yet in the period between 1910 and 1940, their number had been cut in half. No unions were as undemocratic and racist in their policies as the railroad unions; they matched the railroad bosses in every respect.

Finally, the government played a flagrant role in maintaining the anti-Negro policies of the railroads and railroad unions. Here it could clearly be seen that discrimination was not the sole responsibility of the unions but was a *three-party conspiracy* of the government, the railroads, and the unions.

The question of the railroads was a key issue at the third national convention in Chicago in 1953. Coleman Young said in his keynote address:[7]

No industry holds greater drama in the struggle of Negro

Left: Greater New York NLC demonstration to break Jim Crow in the hotel industry.

people, past and present, then does the railroad industry. If this convention, the Negro and white trade unionists and other democratic groups are willing and ready to seize upon this history, upon this drama, we can present to America the most imaginative and far-reaching jobs campaign ever witnessed.

As part of the campaign, an attractive pamphlet called *Let Freedom Ride the Rails* was written, and 50,000 copies were distributed. It eloquently stated the case against the railroads. The NNLC urged Black workers to apply for railroad jobs in the restricted classifications and, in those states with FEPC laws, to report all refusals to the respective State FEPC. Other organizations began to enter the railroad fight. In New York, the State Committee Against Discrimination (official State FEPC) agreed to take up some of the cases the New York NLC was instrumental in having filed.

Cover for Let Freedom Ride the Rails.

One of the most important struggles waged by NNLC was the *Let Freedom Crash the Gateway to the South* campaign, which took place in Louisville, Kentucky, from 1954 to 1956. GE had announced in 1952 that it would move all its appliance factories to Appliance Park, a 700-acre industrial complex, then the largest of its kind, intended to employ 20,000 workers.

Southern leaders of the NNLC thought that this should be taken up by the entire organization. They argued that if Jim Crow was to be broken in the South, the fight would have to begin at the Gateway – Louisville – rather than in the heartlands of oppression. Also, they said, Northern Blacks employed as production workers, who were in unions and had built powerful councils, had a responsibility to use that power to liberate the most oppressed – the brothers and sisters in the South.

The first part of the struggle was waged by the Louisville NLC, which succeeded in influencing the Louisville Board of Education to run classes to train Black people in the skills which would be required in Appliance Park. Trade unionists across the country helped by sending in the job requirements for jobs which they knew would be transferred there.

When GE opened, they met the demand for Black employment with the usual reply that the Blacks were not trained. NNLC was able to settle that argument quickly, because the applicants were trained.

GE grudgingly hired a few Black men on production but refused to hire Black women in any capacity other than matron, despite the fact that the majority of the workers in the plant were to be women. Other companies in the area, Ford and Westinghouse, also discriminated. And all had come to Louisville to take advantage of the Southern differential and lower tax rates. Furthermore, they used the government to subsidize their runaway relocation.

It became increasingly clear that the Louisville NLC needed the all-out support of the other councils across the country.

The Northerners were scared to take on this giant fight. Finally, the leaders decided to meet until they had reached a decision.

This meeting went on for three days while the Southerners sought to allay the fears of their Northern brothers and sisters. One of the big questions was whether it would be possible to raise the money to finance the campaign. Here "Big Train" Thompson once again delivered the goods. He went to UE Local 475 and won their support. He came into the NLC meeting, threw a couple of hundred dollars on the table, and said, "The money's out there, now let's go get it."

Eventually the leaders agreed. On November 10, 1954, the NNLC announced the opening of a drive to win equal job opportunities in the Louisville area. Young pointed out in the press release –

> The right of Negro workers to equal access to production in the South has become a critical test of democracy in America today in view of increasing runaway of big plants from industrial cities in the North.

The NNLC then broke open a national campaign to focus on the Southern differential, the runaway shops, and discriminatory hiring practices, particularly against Black women.

The demand to hire Black women as production workers challenged every racist tradition in the South. Even after companies had hired men, they refused to consider hiring women. NNLC stood firm in its fight for the dignity and economic equality of Black women. In a special pamphlet called "Give us this day our daily bread," they outlined how GE treated women.

The campaign spread from coast to coast as the Black and white masses were mobilized to fight racism in Louisville. With the help of many Black organizations, and the UAW and other unions, two Jim Crow barriers came tumbling down – after twenty years of discrimination, the Louisville Ford plant hired Blacks in categories above janitor, and GE hired some Black women on production. It was the first time in the history of the South that Black women had been hired as factory workers other than matrons.

Pamphlet for NNLC Gateway Campaign. Drawing by Charles White.

7   Repression

No sooner was the NNLC born than it was under attack from the government – Attorney General Brownell, the House Un-American Activities Committee (HUAC), and the Subversive Activities Control Board (SACB), a key McCarthyite institution – and from some white trade unionists who lent themselves to the assault upon progressive ideas.

A basic tenet of the NNLC was that it brought Black workers together in their own organization as a firm base from which they could form alliances with the white brothers and sisters in the labor movement. In a time when Black caucuses were limited to a few progressive unions, NNLC established a forum in which Black workers could come together to deal with their special problems. They established unity with other Black organizations and with white workers to fight on matters of common cause. This was a giant step forward, but it came under attack as "dual unionism" and "rocking the boat." The real basis for the attack upon NNLC was its courageous opposition to all aspects of racism and reaction. Some white union leaders intimidated their members from joining or tried to force them out of NNLC. Others attempted to limit the organization or use it for their own ends.

The government from the beginning set out to destroy NNLC. Brownell attacked it and put it on his "subversive" list. In February 1952, when NNLC had been in operation for three months, Coleman Young and Bill Hood were called before the HUAC. Young was represented by George Crockett, Jr., one of the outstanding lawyers in the United States.

Young said to Crockett, "I want to tell those guys where to go."

"No, Coleman," he was told, "you'd better take the Fifth Amendment." Standard advice in those dangerous days.

They finally compromised. First Young took the Fifth; *then* he told them where to go!

The appearance of NNLC leaders before the committee was an example of fight-back. Before he appeared, Bill Hood said:[8]

> I dare them to put me on the witness stand. I am from Georgia, the same state as the chairman of the un–American Committee, Congressman Wood. I will tell him what I suffered in Georgia – what I saw when I was a young man and which still exists there.

Coleman Young also spoke of the oppression of Black people in the South, and concluded his testimony:[9]

> I am a part of the Negro people. I fought in the last war and I would unhesitatingly take up arms against anybody that attacks this country. In the same manner, I am now in process of fighting against what I consider to be attacks and discrimination against my people. I am fighting against un-American activities such as lynchings and denial of the vote. I am dedicated to that fight, and I don't think I have to apologize or explain it to anybody.

Chairman Wood excused the witnesses. The Southerners who were running the HUAC beat a disordered retreat from Detroit. It was a turning point in the McCarthy terror: Someone had dared to ask, "Who are the real un-Americans?"

Finally, the NNLC was called before the SACB. The Council said:[10]

> If the Attorney General considers the demand for full freedom – economic, political and social – now, not eighty years from now – as subversive, then he had better "designate" the Negro people of America; for this is their demand, and the Negro people are surely "guilty" of fighting for freedom.
>
> And the NLC intends to continue to be "guilty" of fighting for freedom. We will not be intimidated, because the Negro people will not be intimidated. We are fighting for our full freedom, and we do not intend to stop fighting until we can walk with full freedom and dignity in the land of our birth.
>
> We interpret the Attorney General's proposed designation as official notice from "high government sources" that the neo-fascists of America have felt the sting and the fury of our freedom cry. They fear the power of our call to white workers to join with us in our struggle; they are shaken by the growing unity of Negro and white, of the labor movement and the Negro people.

But the NNLC could not withstand the pressure. They faced a frontal attack which would tie up their energies and resources and an attack from the rear by McCarthyite sections of the labor movement. In 1956, the NNLC decided to disband.

The NNLC had, for the first time, brought the skill and power of Black workers into the freedom fight. They had settled the questions of Black power and the right of Black people to have separate organizations, not to build separatism but to build a base from which a coalition could be developed. They had stood firmly on the principle of unity with other Black people and other workers.

As many of the leaders met for the last time on John R Street in Detroit, they wept. They vowed to hold true to the principles of the NNLC, and they pledged to *retreat to the ghetto, build a base there, and come back strong.*

Ernie Thompson fought McCarthyism and he fought racism, but not with 100 percent success. Despite all the years he spent with UE's FPC, there were still some sections of the union where he was not welcome, where Fair Practices was a curse, not a banner.

The forces seeking to destroy the unity of the workers and the militancy and vision of UE and NNLC were powerful. People who remember those times find it hard to explain the fear. They just say, "We were so frightened... It was so scary, you can't imagine."

Ernie had courage, but his voice held a somber note as he spoke to the 1955 UE convention:[11]

> I have a continuous, haunting feeling, an uneasy feeling that perhaps we are not doing quite enough; that somehow, what we are doing is important, not just in itself, but because we are on the threshold in our country of something big – either something democratically better or something much worse.

> We have made a contribution to solving this question of unity. Yet there can be no unity in the United States, and the American labor movement cannot be economically and politically powerful until it is ready and willing to strike down this reign of terror now being launched upon us.

Who but you – the women and the whites who have learned in this union – will stop the reign of terror, will stand by our side?

Let us educate ourselves in this difficult period to stand up in that fight, using our Fair Practices program as our weapon. I think in a large measure democracy and inspiration depend on us here...

Within a year after Ernie said those words, his job with UE ended. The continued assaults upon the union decimated its membership. When, in 1956, the remaining bastions of the UE in the New York-New Jersey area went over to the IUE, Ernie found himself without a base and without a job.

Still the government did not stop its harassment, continually demanding to know why the NNLC should not be added to the Attorney General's list of subversive organizations. Ernie had to borrow money to go to Washington. There he told the government attorneys that they were dancing on the grave of the NNLC.

"How can the dead show cause?" he asked them.

II. RETREAT TO THE GHETTO

As many of the leaders met for the last time on John R Street in Detroit, they wept. They vowed to hold true to the principles of NNLC and they pledged to retreat to the ghetto, build a base there, and come back strong.

Ernest Thompson

8   Gerrymander in Orange Park

ERNIE MOVED TO Orange under protest.

When the idea was first broached, he exploded. "Orange? That's a dirty little Jim Crow town going nowhere. What would I be doing in Orange?"

But Maggie, his second wife, had found a house in Orange for under $10,000. That decided it.

It took a while to establish roots. They were an "odd" family. With a white wife and a "red" union background, Ernie was considered something of a subversive.

He wasn't around much either. Between the UE and the NNLC, he had to do a lot of traveling.

But in 1956 the traveling stopped. Ernie found himself out of a job, in a still strange town, and hemmed into a tight little ghetto.

Mindy, their daughter, was then a second grader at Oakwood Avenue School. The school was segregated and inferior. It was widely known that white students were transferred out and even bused.

The Thompsons learned about this and agreed that Maggie should find a way to inspect the school district map, which was a close-kept secret.

It showed a gerrymander running flagrantly through Orange Park.

"This is a disgrace," said Maggie. "What are we going to do about it?"

"What can we do?" Ernie replied. "We don't have any people or any machinery."

A few days later a neighbor, Thelma Mason, stopped by. She was up in arms about Oakwood, too, but didn't know what could be done. Maggie called Ernie to join the discussion.

"The first thing we have to do if we're going to fight this is to get some people together – neighbors, parents, PTA members – and form a committee," said Ernie.

He asked Thelma to help get it started. She offered to have the first meeting at her house on the following Sunday – January 8, 1958.

The next week was a busy one. Ernie worried that an *ad hoc* committee might fold under the pressure which was sure to come. He wanted to do what he could to ensure that the fight would be won.

He went to see Dr. and Mrs. Benoit Isaac, who had been Orange residents for many years. They were leaders of the Citizens and Taxpayers Association, an established organization that could provide the kind of backing and strength the temporary committee would lack.

Then he went to see Dr. John P. Milligan, head of the New Jersey Division Against Discrimination (DAD) (later the Civil Rights Division), and showed him a map of the gerrymander. Dr. Milligan agreed that a gerrymander existed and urged Ernie to sign a complaint, which he declined to do because that would have put the matter in the exclusive control of the DAD. But he was now reassured that if the people couldn't win this fight on their own, the state was standing in the wings.

The first committee meeting was attended by Preston Grimsley, Harry Smith, Jim and Marge Murphy, Jack and Mary Harrison, Clive Krygar, and others.

Thelma welcomed the other parents and introduced Ernie, who she said, "has had many years of experience in fighting discrimination all across the country and is going to tell us what he thinks about the problem we have here."

Ernie described the discrimination at Oakwood: the bus that carried white children out of the district to the Heywood-Tremont schools; the battered old textbooks relegated to the Black children; the segregation of all Black teachers into Oakwood.

He was able to tell the parents from experience what the possibilities were of winning such a fight. "I think," he summed up, "that we have a case against the board and we can win this go-round."

Others expressed doubts that a group as powerful as the board of education would listen to them.

"I think we can do it," Ernie replied. "First we have to bring it into the light of day – there's no way the board can deny that discrimination exists. We can rally other organizations to support us in demanding that the board explain itself. Then we can up the pressure to force them to change it. The first thing we have to do is form a committee. We must move out in an organized way."

The tradition of fear was deep. Confronting the powerful whites was a risky business. But Ernie was able to reassure them that it was possible to win, and the Committee for More Democratic Schools was formed. Subcommittees were named, including one on the press which was to immediately release to the Orange *Transcript* a story on the gerrymander.

No sooner had the meeting adjourned than the establishment got word of it. A neighbor came around that very night to offer a deal: His daughter and Mindy would be transferred to Lincoln Avenue School if Thompson would keep quiet. Ernie threw him out, saying, "We are not in this fight for ourselves alone. Either we fight for all children or we don't fight. We make no deals with children's futures."

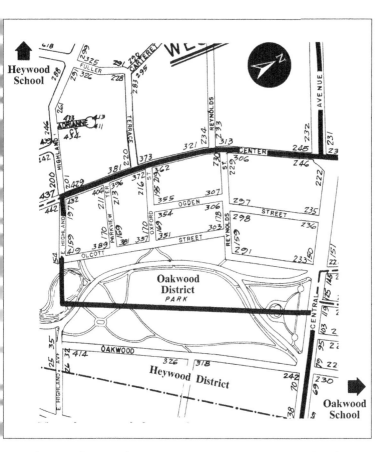

Map of section of Orange showing Jim Crow gerrymander running through Orange Park to permit white children on the east of the park to attend the all-white Heywood Avenue School while zoning Black children on the west of the park into the Oakwood Avenue School.

Word spread that Thompson was a radical and a subversive, and fear was aroused among the members of the committee. One called to say that he had seen the NNLC on the post office list of subversive organizations. He was sorry, but he couldn't be on the committee anymore. Another never said why she dropped out – she just never came around again.

A story was prepared for the press, but everyone on the committee had a good reason why he or she couldn't sign it. Finally, Ernie and Maggie agreed that Maggie would have to do it. Ernie took no chances that the story would be shelved or run on an inside page. He met with the reporters, showed them the map, and convinced them of the existence of injustice. The *Transcript* made it its lead story that week with a banner headline, "BIAS CHARGED IN SCHOOL ZONING."

The newspaper interview charged that the gerrymander had resulted "no less than in the South, in an overwhelmingly all-Negro separate school with inferior facilities for this modern competitive age"; that the board transferred white children from Oakwood to other schools; that no Black teachers or coaches had ever been appointed to the high school; that Oakwood was not a front-line school; and that the city had direct responsibility for *de facto* segregation in Oakwood, since it had created and maintained an all-Black federal housing project adjacent to the school.

It demanded that the gerrymander be wiped out, that Oakwood be brought up to the level of the other schools, that Black teachers be hired throughout the system, including the high school, and that the housing project be integrated.

The town was stunned. Not a copy of the *Transcript* was available by the end of the day. People were asking a lot of questions. They wondered when the gerrymander lines had been drawn and how the board had kept its secret for so long. Many were grateful that the scandalous situation had been brought to light.

But many others were scared, because it was the first time that Black folks in Orange had spoken out. For a while, it was pretty lonely around the Thompson house.

Gradually, people rallied to the committee. Instead of being destroyed, it grew. The members began to agitate for a meeting with the board, which was set for February 11, 1958.

Dr. Benoit Isaac.

The room was packed with forty parents and residents from the Citizens and Taxpayers Association, the Oakwood PTA, and the Committee for More Democratic Schools. The latter presented a bill of particulars:

1. Eliminate the gerrymandered school lines.
2. Make a special effort to integrate Oakwood.
3. Integrate all schools and classes in the system.
4. Make every effort to maintain numerically equal classes in each grade.
5. Allow all children to begin school at the same age.
6. Make an immediate effort to place Black teachers in all public schools, specifically the high school.
7. Assign all children to schools nearest their homes except in cases of overcrowding.
8. Employ qualified professional personnel other than teachers without regard to race, creed, or color.
9. Improve the substandard schools.

They also presented a brochure entitled, "Gerrymander – they did it 'unto the least of these,'" characterizing the gerrymander as "among the crudest and cruelest ever imposed upon the people of Northern New Jersey, both Negro and white."

Dr. Isaac spoke on behalf of the Citizens and Taxpayers Association: "The members of my organization, some boasting as much as forty years of residence in Orange, can attest to this cruel and blatant gerrymander. For many years, we have watched the Green Bus take children living as close as one hundred feet from Oakwood all the way to the other side of town so they might go to a white school..."

Evelyn Isaac, president of the Oakwood PTA, was announced next. When Clare Murray, a white woman board member, heard the word "PTA," she burst out, "Just what I thought. My Negro girls teaching down at Oakwood are behind this!"

Undeterred, Evelyn began. "We say that you have 'done it unto the least of these,' and we mean that you have created an all-Black school which is an inferior school. Our children are not receiving the same education as the white children. The

Evelyn Isaac.

textbooks that our children have are as old as the year 1944 – passed on to Oakwood when they were worn out in the white schools. Some of them are so old they are still predicting that we will soon fly in airplanes. Many have been used by so many children that they are missing five and six pages at a time.

"For a playground, all our children have is asphalt with painted hop-scotch lines. Even the grade of paper is rougher than that used at Heywood. You have made the Black school a 'leftover' school and condemned our children to an inferior education. But we are here to say that that cannot be."

Opposite the Black parents sat the white board members, not one of whom had a child in the public schools. The president, William Howe Davis, complained about the release of information to the press in advance of the board meeting. "I think we can talk these problems out and solve them without further publicity," he said smoothly. "Perhaps a private meeting with a committee of your people and the board..."

Though some committee members agreed, Ernie realized that such a meeting, closed to the public and the press, would play into the hands of the board.

He slipped out of the room to meet with the reporters and leaked the story to them that the DAD was aware of the gerrymander and was standing by to act upon request. He told the press that he had shown the DAD the map and convinced Dr. Milligan that a gerrymander existed. The *Transcript* checked the story and ran it, increasing the pressure on the board.

The additional publicity had another unexpected result: The DAD felt obliged to act without a complaint having been filed. It initiated an investigation, basing its action on a precedent established in Englewood, where a gerrymander had been wiped out by the courts.

The board of education tried to weaken the campaign by forcing the PTA out of the fight, as Ernie had predicted. The Oakwood principal called a meeting and railroaded through a vote supporting the board. Some of the leaders resisted his action, so the board called in the county leadership of the PTA to enforce the pull-out.

But by that time, the battle was in the hands of the state, and even the PTA's withdrawal did not harm the situation. The board of education was still on the carpet.

Following its investigation, the DAD ordered the board to redraw the lines to eliminate the gerrymander. As a result, children from that part of the ghetto lying south of Central Avenue were re-districted into Heywood, effective the following September.

Immediately, the board opened a campaign of intimidation to keep Black parents from sending their children to Heywood. Again, they used the Oakwood principal, who sent around a slip to all children eligible for transfer, saying, "Check one: I plan to attend _Oakwood _Heywood." This move was patently illegal, but it fooled a few parents.

In spite of the intimidation, however, seventy-five children – almost the whole number entitled – transferred.

The DAD also ordered that Black teachers be assigned throughout the city, and the board announced that four-year-old kindergarten would be established in all schools, rather than only Heywood. Some gains resulted for Oakwood, too, including smaller classes once the children south of Central Avenue were transferred. Better books were provided. And the morale of the remaining Black teachers was improved following the assignment of some of their colleagues to other schools.

The DAD refused to act on *de facto* segregation. It was not until some years later, when Kennedy became President, that official pressure was applied to begin to correct this subtler form of discrimination. The DAD in 1958 claimed it had no jurisdiction.

The Committee for More Democratic Schools was unable to continue the Oakwood fight. It had won the first round by appealing to the power of the state because it could not do the job on its own; when the state refused to lend its power any further, the fight had to stop until the people themselves could build their own power.

But this little taste of victory was sweet. It had taken exactly three months – January 8 to April 8. It crystallized a demand by the people for a commission candidate with serious intentions.

It was about this time that folks started to call Ernie "Homeboy," or "Home" for short.

9 The New Day

DURING THE SCHOOL FIGHT another important event occurred in Orange. Brackets were shaping up for the city election, and some white candidates began to search for Blacks to carry their campaigns into the ghetto. Preston Grimsley was invited to one of these meetings and asked Home to go with him. It was a business meeting where whites were discussing who would take charge of which wards and districts.

At one point, a white candidate turned to Home and Preston and said, pointing to another white person, "He'll be in charge of your ward. He'll give you whatever literature you need, some sound equipment, and whatever else you boys have to have to do the job."

Preston didn't seem surprised.

But Home, who had fought Hague in Jersey City, said, "I ain't working under this guy, and furthermore we ain't going to support you unless we know what you stand for. So why don't you come over our way, and we'll arrange a meeting and then we'll let you know if we support you."

The astonished candidate had no choice, since he needed Black support, and he agreed to the meeting.

As Home saw it, this was the way Blacks could see where the white candidates really stood. The Black community had traditionally depended upon the whites for political leadership. They had to see for themselves the bankruptcy of this policy before they would be strong enough to move out on their own.

Orange was dominated by a few ruling families. Challenges to the oligarchy were rarely successful. Political control was tight. The city fathers sat on the boards of the local banks, headed the charities, and controlled the two parties and the commission. William Howe Davis, senior partner in the leading law firm, was president of the Chamber of Commerce and vice-president of the First National Bank, as well as president of the board of education. He had been the mayor for twelve years, from 1942-54. Frank J. Murray, besides being secretary-treasurer of the Hilton Company, was a director of the Orange Savings Bank, a member of the Knights of Columbus and the Orange Elks, had served on the city council and later the commission, and was the mayor for twelve of his twenty-six years in office.

Corruption was an open secret. The working people were powerless, and this was especially true of the Blacks. Their leaders sought to do as much as they could: They had sent Dr. Walter G. Alexander to the State Assembly in the 1920s as the first Black Assemblyman in New Jersey. But all too frequently, the power of the Black leaders depended on the whites and their own economic independence, rather than strength in the ghetto. It was the pattern that whatever machinery existed was in the hands of the Black middle class. The working class was excluded except for its vote.

There were many stories of the undisguised contempt the Black people faced from the white politicians. Walter G. Savage, another long-time commissioner, when asked by a Black person what he would do for them, replied, "I don't have to do anything – all I have to do is give you liquor, and I'll get the vote."

Blacks were confined to the ghetto. Strict real estate practices guaranteed that they could not live where they chose. They did not dream even of going into the white taverns on Central

Samuel A. Horton.

Avenue, the border of the ghetto. As with their school, their recreational facilities were segregated, inferior, or nonexistent.

Home saw this dilemma in 1958 when he called for the meeting in the ghetto with the white politicians. The Isaacs, Dr. John Alexander, Sam Horton, Preston and Mildred Grimsley, and Charles Millis gathered in Dr. Isaac's basement. The white politicians who showed up were questioned as to their position on the issues of the day, including the school fight and Black representation in government. They were exposed, for it became clear they were not willing to fight for the Blacks.

Preston Grimsley.

It was time to find a candidate who *would*. From their ranks, Dr. Alexander ("Doc") seemed the logical choice.

Doc was a general practitioner who was then in the midst of his studies to become a pediatrician. He lived on Parkview Terrace with his wife Emmy Lou and three sons, John, Robert, and Kevin. His family had been doctors for three generations, and this tradition of economic independence had made him

Molly Brown.

fearless. Home later said of him, "I found my special friend when I needed him. He has stood by me, warm and courageous. His deep commitment has kept him on course through these long years and made him not only my friend but a friend to all of Orange."

Doc was asked to become the people's spokesman. He gave careful thought to the many problems involved. He wondered if victory was possible.

Home recounted his experiences in the Hudson County CIO-PAC and how they had put 10,000 workers in motion to support FDR, and of running labor candidates in Hague's bailiwick. Then he said, "We won't be able to build a political machine in these fifty days before election. What we must do is build a movement. We can begin to bring people together to build an organization and lay the basis for the future."

Charles Millis.

Gradually, Doc was convinced and agreed to run. From that point on, everything he had – his time, imagination, resources, the efforts of all his family – was thrown into this first effort to win representation for the people.

A core of people evolved to

carry the main weight of the campaign, including Home, Sam Horton, Wendell Bankston, Henry Maisich, Preston Grimsley, Molly Brown, and Charles Millis. They formed the strategy committee, the main planning body.

An overall Committee for Representative Government was set up to which all of Doc's active supporters belonged. There were also committees on publicity, fund-raising, sound truck and street corner meetings, canvassing and organization, and women.

It was called the "New Day" campaign.

At one of the early strategy meetings, a small group – both working class and middle class – sat around Doc's house drinking coffee and bourbon and discussing the programmatic projections for the campaign and the kind of machinery needed.

"Let's discuss this question of program," Home began. "Do you know the story about the cat and the fox?

"Cat and Fox were talking one day and the cat said, 'What you gonna do when the dogs come, Mr. Fox?'

"'Oh, that's no problem, no problem at all,' said the fox. 'I got me a boatload of tricks. I'll just do my tricks. One of 'em will work. What you gonna do?'

"'Well,' said the cat, 'I only got one trick – up the tree. I hide in the tree where the dogs can't get me.'

"Just then the dogs came running up, barking and yapping, tearing after the fox and the cat. The cat went up the tree, and though the dogs leaped and strained, they couldn't get him. The fox, down at the bottom of the tree, started doing his tricks. But that didn't save him. Dogs got him and ate him up. Cat shook his head and said, 'It don't pay to know too many tricks.'

"Now, we have to be like the cat and go up the tree – the programmatic tree. We have to base ourselves on program. If you try to be too tricky when you mess with the Man, he'll

Up the Programmatic Tree, by Rich Brown.

give you cards and spades and big casino every other hand, and still beat you. If you want to win, you got to stay with the tree.

"We'll be like the cat" – he brushed his palms together, one up, one down – "and go up the tree."

Having established the central role, Home turned to its contents. "Our program has to highlight the major issues of the day, whatever you think they are – relocation, unemployment, the schools. It should emphasize the major problem. Right now, I think that's the Freeway."

Discussion slowly clarified the issues. Some were concerned that the Freeway, an East-West super-highway which was cutting across the ghetto, be a depressed road, which was a safer and more aesthetic solution than an elevated highway. Others raised the need for aid in relocation. There existed no plan to help families dispossessed by the Freeway.

"We should develop a main programmatic piece of literature which will present our whole program, and then we should develop special pieces on issues which are key – such as this relocation business. But the central task at this point is to get the issues straight and set them out so the voters will know where we're coming from," Home emphasized.

Home brought the meeting back to the schools. "Even though we won the fight on the Oakwood gerrymander, there is still a lot to be done. There are nothing but old schools in Orange; they need to be modernized or rebuilt. There still are no Black teachers or coaches in the high school. And there's nobody Black on the board of education. I think we have to stick with our slogan of 'unto the least of these.' Even though a few of our children are now going to Heywood, we must not forget those left at Oakwood.

"Paul Robeson taught me this lesson. When I met Paul, I was a foundry worker and he was a famous college student

HOME-COMING BARBECUE

IN HONOR OF

New Jersey's Best Known Son

PAUL
ROBESON

SUNDAY, JULY 29, 1956

2:00 P. M.

AT THE HOME OF

Ernest & Margaret Thompson

397 Olcott Street, Orange, N. J.

Horseshoe Pitching ● Ping Pong

COME ONE!   COME ALL!

WELCOME PAUL HOME AND HAVE FUN

at Rutgers and an All-American halfback. His brother was a pastor in Bayonne and Paul used to go visiting with us on Sunday afternoons. He would sing, and we would sing, and all of us would have fun.

"Years later when Paul went into the theatre and on the concert stage, I often went to see him perform. Then, by standing invitation, I would go backstage. Paul, surrounded by celebrities and the press, would look over the crowd and see me – the foundry worker. He would excuse himself and say, 'Ernie, come here. Gee, it's good to see you, fellow. Stay around and we'll talk.'

"Time and again Paul went out of his way to make me feel 'You're somebody.' He taught me the dignity of 'the least of these.' This has been my guide. The

Paul Robeson talking with Mindy at the Thompson home in early 1956.

need is to extend this concept so that it is embraced by the Black middle class."

They finally summed up the issues that were to make up the New Day platform: redevelopment and relocation, unemployment, the Freeway, the school system, civil rights, recreation and juvenile delinquency, and representative government.

As it turned out, this became an outline not only for the New Day campaign but for the years of struggle to come.

10 The Campaign Rolls

HOME BEGAN TO TEACH people about how to run a campaign. "The main lesson I learned over the years in watching the Hague machine is the lesson of the canvass," said Home. "In Jersey City during Hague's day, his workers canvassed every house before election day. They took their literature directly to the voters to find out whether they were Democrats, Republicans, or uncommitted. Then they went back on election day to every Democrat and made sure he got out to vote, and did the same with uncommitted people if they felt there was a chance to move them.

"In this way, your program has gone out to all the voters and you have a chance to tell them what you're for, which you can't always do through mass meetings or the sound truck. This is the only way to ensure that your message reaches the voters.

"Now, I don't think we will be able to canvass the whole city, but we should try to cover the whole ward. This ghetto is our base and this is where we can expect to make a strong showing. We'll hit the other parts of the city if and when we can."

These ideas were batted around for a while. How many houses could one person canvass? How could they get lists of registered voters? How could they sign up volunteers to do the job? How many election districts and polling places were there? Where could they expect to pick up votes outside the ward? These were only a few of the questions that had to be answered in deciding their first election strategy.

It was a challenge, but the excitement began to grow. With the New Day on the scene, the old methods, where the middle class acted independently in its own interest, no longer went unchallenged.

It was discussed repeatedly in the strategy committee that the campaign was in the hands of not one class but two – the middle-professional class *and* the working class. This coalition was the basis for success. The majority of Black men and women held jobs in factories, service, or clerical work. They were workers, not middle class. Of necessity, they were disciplined in a way the middle class was not. They understood the power of the people; they knew about coalition; they knew how to fight. In addition, it had to be understood by all that they fought for the whole community.

The old middle-class method of work died with an experience of Doc's. It had been suggested to him that he go see a white politician and ask for his help. Doc thought it was a good idea and promised to do so. When he brought it up at a strategy meeting, Home said to him, "What are you going to tell the Man?"

Doc said, "I'm going to point out to him that the Black community is now united and *Strong Men* are comin' on. We deserve representation, which we have long been denied, and I hope he will help me win the election."

"I'll bet around the board," said Home, "that right now I can make the speech Mr. Charlie's going to make to you. I'll tell you how it's going to go. He's going to say what Churchill said, that he didn't come to preside over the liquidation of the empire. Mr. Charlie isn't going to crack a smile. He'll just look at you, and finally you're going to reach for your hat. When you do that, he's going to smile on you and think, 'Now this boy knows his place.'

"Then he's going to let you know he is not going to change anything one iota, that you can do this and you can do that – which will leave you right where you are this minute. Because we haven't shown any strength or power, and why should Mr. Charlie *give* us some?"

Doc nevertheless went ahead with the meeting.

The next night at the strategy meeting the committee wanted to know if Home had been right.

Doc said, "He sure was!" He described what happened: "Well, I made my pitch like I said I would, and Mr. Charlie looked at me stern and said nary a word. I kept talking and he kept listening. Man, I finally reached for my hat and said, 'Some friends thought it would be a good idea if I asked you for your help in my campaign.' Then Mr. Charlie reared back and smiled for the first time. He figured I knew my place. Well, he gave me a spiel on what I might do, but he never offered to raise a finger."

Home said, "You cats pay me my money and let Doc and the rest of us learn one more lesson. Did you ever hear the story about big, bad Mr. Lion?

"One morning the sun was shining pretty. Mr. Lion came out and started down the path, and he ran into Rabbit. He said, 'Rabbit, who's the King of the Jungle?' and he let out a mighty roar. Rabbit shook all over and said, 'You are, mighty Lion.'

"Then Lion went a little farther and ran into Antelope. He roared, 'Antelope, who's the King of the Jungle?' Antelope shook all over, said 'You are, great Lion,' and started running.

"Just around the corner, Lion ran into Elephant. He was feeling good by that time, and he roared at Elephant, 'Who's the King of the Jungle?' Elephant picked him up and threw him against the trunk of a tree. When Lion had gathered his battered self together and licked his bruises, he said, 'You didn't have to get so mad, just because you didn't know!'"

As the laughter subsided, Home summed up, "Doc, Strong Man is coming, but he ain't made the scene yet, so we'll let Mr. Charlie slide this time 'cause he didn't know."

Armed with a program, the campaign went into the streets through canvassing, street corner meetings, and constant use of the sound truck. Literature was put out that sought to answer the community's questions. The involvement of the people around a Black candidate, on a program worked out by Blacks, was a new departure in Orange politics. From the beginning of the campaign, the leaders sought to give it character and strength by drawing on the culture and history of Black people, signified in music and poetry. "Strong men comin' on, strong men gittin' stronger" became the traveling verse.

The campaign was launched on April 10 at a mass meeting at Union Baptist Church. Its pastor, Reverend J. Vance McIver, was master of ceremonies. There were many endorsements, including Evelyn Isaac for the Citizens and Taxpayers Association; Evelyn Ennis, president of Oakwood PTA; Clive Krygar for the Committee for More Democratic Schools; and John Gallagher, legislative director of Local 467, IUE, who spoke on coalition of labor and blacks.

Finally, Rudy Thomas introduced the candidate, who told the gathering movingly what the New Day campaign stood for. Doc "walked that walk and talked that talk."

Involving women in the work was a conscious policy from the beginning. Throughout the campaign, women played the most decisive role in raising funds, working at the polls, and supplying the dominant mood of enthusiasm. They kept their pledge to canvass, and they held a tea where over $1,000 was raised.

Even children caught the excitement of the campaign. Every afternoon as they came from school, they stopped at the headquarters at Oakwood and Central for buttons and leaflets to hand out. Some of those who lived in Doc's neighborhood, including Mindy Thompson, wrote and distributed their own programmatic piece:

ELECT DR. JOHN W. ALEXANDER FOR COMMISSIONER

because –

We need bigger and better parks and playgrounds

We need more homes for people who will lose their homes when the Freeway is built

We need better schools, too

So pitch in and win... Let's have a better city

Issued by:

Children for Dr. Alexander

As the campaign gained momentum, red-baiting opened up on Home. During the campaign Doc had to go to Atlantic City to take his pediatric examinations. While he was away, Rudy Thomas came to see Home, telling him that he had heard that somebody had a story "exposing" the communists in the campaign.

As soon as Doc got back, Home told him what had gone on. Doc wanted to know what it was all about. "Tell it to me straight, man. Why are they trying to wreck my campaign by attacking you?"

Home told him, "Your campaign is the first step in challenging the old-line politics and politicians. We are opening the fight for Black representation and a role for labor and women in running this city. We are bound to come under attack. Mr. Charlie isn't going to step aside peacefully and let you take over.

"I come to this fight with a sworn commitment. My job for many years was to help break Jim Crow in shops across the country. I am one of the proud Black working sons who were part of the vital labor movement of the '40s, and I have been trained in organizing, negotiating, and programming.

"In addition, I come embodying the culture of our people. I cut my eye teeth on Dunbar, and I have never forgotten the stories told me by my grandfather, who had been a slave. Our culture and a fierce love of our dignity will be the main weapons in the battle that is coming.

"These are the elements the New Day needs. If they split you off from me, who will supply these new elements?"

After careful thought, Doc answered, "I will *not* be intimidated by false issues. *We* will henceforth pick our leaders."

The campaign built symbols and forged bonds between the Black working class and the middle-professional class. But there were other problems. The key questions were: How was a powerless minority to achieve effective power? How was the coalition to be extended throughout the city?

Alliances were sought with white candidates. The committee approached those who did not have full tickets of five and attempted to get them to run with Alexander, the only Black person in the field. To a man, they refused.

About the same time, Home began to hear a persistent rumor that the Alexander forces were peddling Vote Black — a bullet vote campaign. A bullet vote means that a voter having a certain number of votes (five in this case) casts his ballot for only one candidate, deliberately sacrificing his other four votes to increase his candidate's margin.

Home brought the matter before the strategy committee. One of the leaders who favored the tactic defended it, "Alexander is the Black man's candidate and therefore the Black people should vote for him. You yourself have said that the whites don't represent us or fight for our interests. Why should we vote for them? We should go all out to vote Black. Show the whites we mean business."

"Do you know how to count?" Home asked. "Do you want to play games — or win an election? You can't win with the bullet vote because that will attract only Black votes, and there simply aren't enough Black votes in town. It's not an emotional question. If you want a piece of this action, let's forget the bullet vote."

Doc backed Home. "We're only 20 percent of the population and even if we got all the Blacks, that wouldn't put us in the running. Besides, if we really want to show the Man that *Strong Man* has come on the scene, we can show him even better by hitting him hard in his own wards. Our program is in the interests of all the citizens of Orange, and I think we can win white votes to support it."

Home explained that the rumor "is the work of the Man to isolate Alexander from the white voters. He needs it to make sure we don't make progress. I have seen this time and again where whites peddled this jive hoping to bury a candidate in the Vote Black trap. Now they hope to bury Doc. At the same time, they're probably moving out to scare the Blacks away from us 'separatists' and get the votes for themselves!"

"O.K., Home, if what you say is true, then what shall we do about it?" asked Millis.

"We have to take Alexander out of isolation. Even though the whites won't run with him, we can support four of them on an independent basis. This would put to rest the Vote Black charge and give us a greater basis for moving ahead in the white wards."

The argument went on for two weeks. When all the members of the committee had become convinced, they examined the field, had discussions with representatives of organized labor, and independently selected and endorsed four white candidates to make up a five-man slate with Alexander. They then campaigned for all five, although – with one exception – the white candidates were afraid to support Alexander.

This was not coalition: It was a protective move to prevent the slaughter of Alexander, and an offensive move to influence the outcome of the election on a city-wide basis. They made the move independently, without commitments from the white candidates. They would cooperate with the whites to the extent the whites would permit; the whites owed them nothing.

The only whites in Orange who understood coalition and were willing to unite with Blacks were in the labor movement. Labor had learned this lesson, as had Home, during the Roosevelt years and the rise of the CIO, the greatest coalition yet seen in America. The campaign turned to labor for support, and a coalition was established with sections of labor.

The Essex-Hudson CIO Council endorsed Doc. Rudy Thomas and Harold Smith, who had worked with Home over the years in UE and NNLC, were active in Local 467, IUE. Rudy went after support of the local for Doc. The local cooperated in the selection of such white candidates as were endorsed; it invited Doc to appear at membership meetings; it lent the use of its headquarters for special campaign affairs; and it put people to work for Doc because his program was one which would benefit all the people. Special leaflets were issued by Doc appealing for labor support.

The campaign grew in all directions, closing with two big events. One was a super-rally at Local 467's hall. The other was a motorcade led by "Seneca" Charles Millis. Millis owned a big red buckskin. Riding Buck and dressed in his tribal garb, Millis led the cars through the length and breadth of town. The parade ended at the Thompson house for one of Proctor Malone's famous barbecues.

On election day, May 13, 1958 – fifty days after Doc made his decision to run – the campaign manned every polling place in the city with two volunteer workers apiece. When the polls closed, the workers reported to Dr. Isaac's basement.

Doc did not win, but he ran exceedingly well, better than any Black candidate had ever done in Orange. He led all candidates in his ward, and two of the whites supported by his campaign were victorious. What was most important for the long haul were the strides taken toward building the ward into a political stronghold for Blacks.

The people wanted to continue. Before they adjourned that night, they pledged to form a permanent organization.

The building of power for the powerless was on its way.

NEW DAY FOR ORANGE
– ELECT –

Dr. John W. Alexander
FOR COMMISSIONER

Vote for Representative Government

Vote Number **9**

TUESDAY   MAY 13th

New Day Platform

I. REDEVELOPMENT AND RELOCATION
   1. The partial redevelopment plan now under consideration must be implemented to include other sections of the City in order to increase ratables and improve the character of the city.
   2. Study future water needs based on the projected plans.
   3. A Citizens Committee be set up to work side by side with the City Commissioners to bring in private housing capital and industry.
   4. Seriously examine the need to replace the ancient City Hall.

II. UNEMPLOYMENT
   1. Problems resulting from the current recession and shops leaving our City must be vigorously met by the City officials.
   2. Unemployment Compensation should be extended and increased immediately as was done in the state of New York.
   3. Federal taxes should be immediately reduced to increase the purchasing power of consumers and relief to business.
   4. Maximum distribution of federal surplus food supplies to the unemployed and others in need.
   5. The maximum use of local labor forces in the Redevelopment program and other government projects should be mandatory.
   6. The efficiency of the Welfare Department and its service to the people should be studied for maximum benefits to be obtained.

III. FREEWAY
   1. It should be the policy of the City Government, which is not now the case, to provide all aid and assistance in relocation of the displaced families.
   2. An official city committee should be established whose duties it shall be to provide relocation and assistance.
   3. Depress the Freeway to protect the properties and beauty of the City.

VI. SCHOOL SYSTEM
   1. Discriminatory school lines still in existence in Orange and all other forms of discrimination in the school system should be wiped out.
   2. Federal funds should be sought for the purpose of improvement of the physical plants.
   3. Adequate pay for teachers and other city employees.
   4. Strengthen the school system by amending the charter to permit an elected Board of Education.

V. CIVIL RIGHTS
   1. The City of Orange should have a functioning Civil Rights Committee.

VI. RECREATION AND JUVENILE DELINQUENCY
   1. Develop and implement a year-round recreational program thru-out the City.
   2. Establish a special division in the Police Department manned by trained personnel to develop a program to prevent and manage Juvenile Delinquency.

VII. REPRESENTATIVE GOVERNMENT
   1. The future of Orange is contingent upon achieving these objectives through representative government made up of Negroes and Whites.

11   Building Power

IN THE DAYS FOLLOWING the election, Home and Doc planned for the future. Home heard rumors that some people wanted to call the new organization the John Alexander Association. Though it was traditional to name the political machinery after the candidate, it was another hangover from the past.

"Doc," he explained, "we have to make it clear from the beginning that this is a people's organization. We want the name to reflect that commitment. The machinery we build must be firmly in the hands of the people."

Doc strongly agreed. When the idea came up at the first organizational meeting, Home took the floor. "What we want," he reminded them, "is to carry on the work we have begun in the New Day campaign. There we fought for representation for Black people in government, and for programs that dealt with the problems of all the city. We called ourselves the Committee for Representative Government – government that answers the needs of the people. That's what we have to continue. I move that we call this organization 'Citizens for Representative Government,' in line with our commitment."

The name was adopted and the issue of representation came to the floor. There were no Black faces in City Hall in any job category. There were no Blacks on the board of education. There were no Black teachers or coaches in the high school.

To impact school districting lines, housing relocation, and

other problems of the ghetto, it was clear they had to go to the central arena, City Hall, and use their new power there.

The first organizational action of Citizens for Representative Government (CRG) was to designate the Housing Authority, the Board of Education, and City Hall as key places to fight for representation. Through negotiations in the months that followed, Blacks gained representation on the Housing Authority in the person of Dr. Isaac. They threw their weight behind the appointment of two labor representatives to the same body. Colson Woody, with CRG backing, became the first Black member of the board of education.

Home felt that they had to take partisan action, too. The Democratic Party in the ward was not representative. Although the ward was 75 percent Black, there were only two Black committee people out of twelve.

In the primaries that spring, Sam Horton had independently run a county committee slate of six Blacks, including Preston and Mildred Grimsley, against the Democratic line. All but one had been defeated. After the election, it was discovered that the woman who had run against Mildred Grimsley had moved out of town prior to the election. Preston protested to the Superintendent of Elections, charging fraud.

Ovid Colalillo, Orange Democratic chairman and law partner of then Congressman Hugh J. Addonizio, retorted, "Our district leaders are doing a good job, white or Negro. Grimsley's organization ran six Negroes against our leaders in the last election, and five of them lost. The voters of Orange decide these issues."

Home, Doc, the Grimsleys, Horton, and a few others, in response to this discrimination by the Democrats, demanded a meeting with Colalillo. He refused.

They contacted Congressman Addonizio, County Chairman

Dennis F. Carey, and Governor Robert B. Meyner. They told them that the party was not representative, that the city chairman refused to meet with them, and that if something was not done, they might have to oppose the party in November. They put forward the demand: seven to five, or fight.

The Democrats were then fighting for control in Essex County after fifty years of Republican domination. They needed all the support they could get, so Addonizio agreed to arrange the meeting with Colalillo. But the Blacks insisted that Addonizio also be present; they refused to meet without him since he was running for re-election and would be more responsive to their arguments. He at last agreed and the meeting took place.

Addonizio opened by saying, "We understand what your complaints are, but we stand fully behind what Colalillo said – that the voters will decide who will represent them. If you want representation on the committee, then you should go out and get it. And we will do all we can to ensure that you get a fair election."

"We will meet you, Congressman, but not when you think we will," Home replied. "We know as well as you do that the names designated on the party line will probably be elected in the spring primaries. We want Black people designated on that line. Seven Blacks to five whites. Plus the chairmanship of the ward. Seven to five, or we will meet you – in November."

In November, they knew, the defection of one ward with a large voter turnout might cast the balance to the Republicans. Addonizio didn't like the sound of that. "Look, this isn't something to get all hot about. I'm sure we can come to some settlement. Perhaps it could be worked out so that some of your people would be designated on the line. But seven to five is out. How about an even split – six to six?"

Some of the delegation thought this sounded good and started to move for it.

But Home, sitting in the corner, closed his eyes and shook his head. "No, no. No days like that. With six to six, Colalillo will pick the chairman, and it will be Colalillo's man, not our man. That cannot be. We Black Democrats will control the operation of the party in the ward of Black majority. Seven to five plus the chairmanship is the way the deal has to go down."

Addonizio knew he needed the votes of this Black ward which had shown so strongly for Alexander. He agreed to the demand, seven to five plus the chairmanship, in exchange for support in the ward.

With the Democratic designation for seven Blacks, CRG-sponsored candidates won the posts, and Preston Grimsley was elected to ward chairmanship in April 1959. It was the first time in the history of Orange that a Black had become a ward leader, and one of the first two times in the state; simultaneously, Eulis C. ("Honey") Ward became the leader of the Democratic Party in Newark's Central Ward.

In the November election, the Democrats took leadership of Essex County but their plurality was less than the East Ward's majority. CRG and the Democratic Party took note of this significant event.

The Black Democrats in Orange extended their efforts. Their Orange Progressive Democratic Coordinating Committee worked with others in the Essex County Negro Democratic Committee for Recognition, which presented these demands:

1. Equal representation on committees.
2. Equal voice in selection of candidates.
3. Equality of jobs in all categories.
4. Greater Black representation for elective office, from county committee to Congress.

With these two building blocks – CRG and control of the

Democratic Party in the ward – they laid a concrete basis for moving into the central arena. The machinery was firmly in the hands of the people; CRG leadership and the party posts were held by the working class, who were the majority in the community, to ensure that whatever power was achieved would be used in the interests of all.

12 Into the Central Arena

ONE OF THE PLANKS of the New Day campaign was a pledge to fight for charter change – a change in the city's form of government from commission to something more representative. Orange was one of the few remaining New Jersey cities which had not abandoned the archaic commission form, which required the at-large election of all representatives.

The Alexander campaign had reaffirmed that it was practically impossible for women, Blacks, or other minorities to be elected. The Black community knew that Alexander was the best candidate in the field in 1958 and the only one with a program for all the people. But he could not win. It was the consensus that no candidate could be elected without the endorsement of the power structure in Orange.

The form of government, then, had to be changed to make it possible to have a Black representative. Change would also benefit the whole city by enabling the citizens to have more direct control over their government. In order to effect this change, CRG had to leave the ghetto and move out into the city as a whole to win the support of large sections of the white community.

By late 1958, various moves had been made that interested some white liberals. Hearing of this, a reporter for the *Transcript* went to see what he could learn. He found Preston Grimsley, who told him, "Well, yes, the people in our ward are interested in charter change and have been organizing on this question. We hope to go out all over the city and get people involved in this because we think that charter change is what the city needs. And we are willing to lead the fight to get it."

That was all the reporter needed to hear. In the next issue of the *Transcript,* there was a big article telling how the Blacks wanted charter change, that it was a Black thing. The article in effect told the whites to watch out; otherwise they would end up with a Black person in City Hall.

When the whites who had been involved heard this, they got scared and ran. The basis for the coalition had not been strong to begin with. And the whites were not prepared to hear that they were being led by Blacks in order to put a Black person in government. They quickly pulled out, and CRG was left with the pieces.

When Doc and Home got hold of Preston, Home told him, "Look, Preston, you shouldn't have made that statement. You didn't even consult before you made it. There's always going to be reporters around asking what you think of this and that. That doesn't mean that you, one, have to go off and give them answers. You got to find out what the outlook is before anything is said.

"See, Preston, big talk don't buy you nothing but trouble."

"I can see that now," Preston conceded. "What can we do next?"

"Well, we'll have to start over. But I think that we have to make sure that this time we don't make no mistakes. *We* aren't going to go out in front and be a target for the Man. We're going to have to find some whites who are interested in the issue and willing to take the lead. Then we can come in once the coalition is off the ground. But we can't be the first to move out if we're going to avoid setting up a target for the Man. And that's an easy target: 'The Blacks want to get greedy.' He'll use it every time. So first of all, we got to find some whites to lead off.

"At this point, we have to go after the keys. We don't have contact with all the whites, but we can go to the keys – leaders in the Democratic Party and the labor movement. We can get them to go after their members and bring them into the struggle. There's also a possibility that some of these Republicans who are out of power might be interested in a piece of the action and we can cruise them along."

"Republicans?" Preston asked.

"Why not? They got some people, see? You got to understand that if you want something, sometimes you have to make coalition with the devil in order to get it. I don't mean that we're going with him all the way down the road. But we can use Republican support to win this charter change. We're going to need all the help we can get."

For the next two years, the leaders of CRG worked to get whites involved and to encourage them to move the campaign out. Finally, by 1961, enough people had been collected so that the whites thought they could begin; a meeting was called to establish the Charter Change Association. Ambrose Hardwick, a Republican and retired executive, became president. Three CRG leaders, including Home, were elected to the board. The big questions were how to develop interest in the campaign and what legal steps were necessary.

Lawyers were called in to outline the legal problems. The first was to have a Charter Change Commission elected. CRG independently examined the possibilities and developed a slate of candidates which they presented to the Democratic Party. They then fought within the Charter Change Association to have that slate put on the ballot.

The petition campaign got underway, and the Black

community threw its organized machinery behind it. The issue was placed on the ballot for November 7, 1961, and the Charter Study Commission was elected. The first round had been won.

The job of the commission was to review the old form of government, consider proposed forms, and suggest in a report to the citizens what changes would be appropriate. There would then be a vote on their proposal, and the voters would decide whether to change the government.

Hearings were set up in various parts of town and individuals and organizations invited to attend. CRG felt that it was not enough to want to change the government: There had to be something better to change to. They agreed on mayor-council form and actively organized support for it by getting other groups in the city to come to the hearings.

The commission report, issued in April 1962, stated:

> The basic weaknesses (of commission form of government) include the fusion of legislative and administrative powers in the same hands... This condition fosters delay, 'trading' and personal politics... does not afford the opportunity for sound budgeting and planning... makes impossible a unified public policy... not only violates the principle of checks and balances but also prevents an independent review of the actions of the governing body.

They recommended a mayor-council plan, with a council consisting of seven members to be elected every four years at a non-partisan election, three at-large and one from each of four wards – East, West, North, and South.

The vote on the commission's recommendation was put on the ballot for June 1962.

The city election for a new commission was coming up in May.

Concern grew that it would detract from the very important charter change election in June. Already several Blacks were talking about running for the commission.

"We're going to need all our strength to fight for charter change, and so we have to do everything possible to unify our forces," Home said. He suggested that CRG propose a boycott of the commission elections.

"There isn't any way that a Black candidate can win at-large. So we might as well boycott, and that will save money and time that can be put into the change fight."

"I hear that Bill Cook and Ray Murphy are planning to run," said Millis, shaking his head. "Those are going to be some tough guys to convince not to run. Bill Cook don't listen to nobody and Ray Murphy isn't too friendly. We had a hard time even getting his organization to testify at the charter change hearings."

Home also suggested that CRG support the white candidates who were in favor of charter change. "If they win, it will be easier for change to win. Nick Franco has come out in support of change, and David Feisner, and I think some others. The stronger the showing we have now, the better will be our position in the June election. I would like to propose a slogan for this campaign: that we put all our eggs in the change basket, not spread them around."

"What if we drop the basket?" someone asked.

"If we don't win charter change, we won't have any eggs anyway," Millis replied.

Both Cook and Murphy, however, rejected the idea of boycott.

Murphy called Home one night and said, "I'd like to come and talk to you."

Home said, "Fine." Murphy had been sponsored by CRG for

a post on the Housing Authority and was considered a friend.

To Home's surprise, he showed up with a small committee including a young woman named Rebecca Doggett.

"I've come to see you," began Murphy, "because I wanted to announce that I'm running for commission in May – even if Alexander runs. My organization and I think I could best represent the people of this ward."

"Ray," Home answered, "you know that Doc isn't going to run. We're asking all Black candidates to boycott the election and prepare for the vote on charter change in June. Charter change is just gaining strength. A setback now might destroy the movement and indefinitely postpone Black representation in Orange. Even with citywide support and the best program, Alexander couldn't win in 1958. I don't see how you think you can win now. Why don't you wait for the change?"

"It doesn't matter if we don't win this election. It will be a good opportunity to mobilize the Black community. Dr. Alexander went for citywide support, but we're building our thing here. We want Black votes, not white votes."

Home explained that this was a hopeless tactic in Orange. "We're not talking about Newark, where there's a boatload of Black folks. We're talking about Orange. We don't think that any Black can win citywide at this time. Besides, if we win the charter change, there will be a councilman elected from this ward. I would be willing to fight for support for you in that election, and with the backing of our organization plus your own, you would be guaranteed a seat as the first Black councilman."

"We don't buy your stalling. We have decided that we are the ones to lead the ward. We don't have any respect for your leadership, and I'm stepping forward to represent the Black people of this ward," Murphy declared.

"You may or may not respect our leadership, but you better respect facts. And the facts are that without coalition, without any support from whites, you – a Black man – can't win against the overwhelming white majority. Coalition is based on common cause, not bowing down to the whites. And it's the only way you can win in a town like this."

But Murphy and his friends had already moved to put on their hats and coats. Rebecca Doggett lingered behind and obviously wanted to talk further, but she was hustled out the door.

CRG eventually decided to support Murphy in the commission race, though they were positive he would be defeated. After their endorsement, they met with his campaign committee and tried to convince them to support some white candidates who were in favor of charter change, but Murphy was hopelessly committed to a Vote Black tactic and refused to listen.

Candidates opposed to charter change won easily, taking four seats. Murphy lost decisively. Franco won but was left in a precarious position since he was the only pro-change candidate who did win. One other white candidate who was pro-change would probably have won had he had Murphy's support. The city paid a heavy price for Murphy's Vote Black policy.

CRG immediately started its preparations for the June referendum and this time succeeded in gaining the cooperation of the Murphy organization, which belatedly accepted the importance of charter change.

Up against the Old Guard of white politicians, who expected to win, CRG based its campaign on a special effort to get a high turnout of the registered voters in the East Ward. Day after day, using sound trucks, leaflets, and canvassers, they told the community that all their hopes and dreams were riding on their votes, and they said it over and over and over. Ernie's younger son Josh, who was then five, rode with him in the sound truck so often he could do a perfect imitation of his, "This is your Town Crier... It's change time..."

The opposition ran an anti-Black campaign. Their message was, "Do you want a nigger in City Hall?" The racism became so vicious that the Orange Association for Charter Study organized and ran an advertisement by prominent citizens denouncing the ugly tactic.

Under the leadership of the citywide coalition, the referendum passed by the narrow margin of sixty-five votes. A key to victory was the Black ward, where the voter turnout was increased by four percent although the vote in special elections is generally far smaller than in regular elections.

All things being equal, the establishment should have won, but they took it for granted that they had the election in the bag.

CRG took nothing for granted. And won.

13 Gerrymander Again

DURING THE CHARTER change fight, while all of CRG's forces were tied up, the *Transcript* published a map which revealed that the board of education had established a new gerrymander. All the Black Oakwood students were sent to Central Elementary School, creating a Jim Crow school in the heart of the main white business district. Central's white students were siphoned off into Park Avenue School.

Before CRG could mobilize, the situation broke in an unexpected way. Park Avenue parents began to demand a gym and a cafeteria. In retaliation, the board issued an order sending their seventh and eighth grades back to Central. The Park Avenue parents rebelled. They marched on a board meeting to demand that the order be rescinded, offering to drop their demand for school improvements. Doc and Home listened to this anti-Black business at the meeting.

Doc eventually had a chance to speak. "The Orange Board of Education is sitting here high and mighty and using naked blackmail to intimidate the Park Avenue parents.

"And you parents are just as guilty. When you say you don't want your children walking long distances or going to an inferior school, you are really saying you don't want them to go to school with Black children.

"The board is using your anti-Black feelings to deny your children things they should have.

"But the real victims of this blackmail are not the children at Park Avenue School. They are not you parents. They are not the members of the board. The real victims are the Black children gerrymandered into an inferior school and denied the kind of education they need!"

It was like a bolt of lightning. The parents were furious at being accused – some were liberal whites who didn't like to think of themselves as racist. The board denied it was talking blackmail. It insisted there was not enough room at Park Avenue for the extra facilities unless "some sacrifices were made."

CRG immediately opened a fight on the gerrymander. This time they were stronger and more experienced. They held a public meeting at Union Baptist Church, to which they invited a speaker from the national office of the NAACP, who put the heat on the local chapter to come into the fight. Agreement was reached to work jointly on demands that included Oakwood as well as Central. A white paper was issued describing the gerrymander and demanding:

1. a public hearing;
2. desegregation of Oakwood and Central by the end of 1961;
3. the closing of classes at Oakwood, moving the administrative office from Colgate to Oakwood, and reopening classes at Colgate.

The board finally acted favorably on the Central gerrymander but still refused to take action on Oakwood. CRG found this unacceptable, but its hands were tied since the NAACP had taken the case to the United States District Court. In court, the board's lawyer argued that the NAACP had not exhausted administrative remedies and that the case had to go to the Commissioner of Education. He prevailed and the case was dismissed. A hearing was held before the commissioner, who found Orange guilty of *de facto* segregation and fined the city a quarter of a million dollars in state aid, pending the end of segregation. The board failed to take any action until convinced the commissioner meant business. An open enrollment proposition was then adopted, which did not satisfy anybody, but which the commissioner allowed for one year.

In the meantime, William Braun, president of the board, made a public statement in a civil rights hearing in Newark to the effect that there might be "congregation," but there was no "segregation" in Orange. He further stated that the Black people were satisfied with conditions in the schools and that the NAACP was a "self-styled" leader in the school struggles.

"This guy has got to go," Home said. "We will not get any real improvement in education until he is off the board."

Millis burst out: "We ought to blast him to the moon for saying we 'congregate' in the worst housing in the city. What does he think we are – fools?"

"We have to take this to the streets," Doc added. "And then we'll have to continue the fight to get *all* those people off the board and get some people on who care what happens to the children of Orange."

An *ad hoc* committee called One Voice for a Democratic Orange was formed. The campaign began with petitions, letters to the *Transcript* from both white and Black citizens, advertisements by prominent citizens, a white paper, and a letter to numerous white residents explaining the campaign to remove Braun.

An open letter was sent to Braun:

> We, the undersigned, openly express to you our
> sincere and anguished indignation at your recent public
> statements before the Civil Rights Commission of the

United States government…

In your invocation of a defense that 90 percent of the Negroes in Orange are 'satisfied' with present education facilities, you bring to mind the slave owners of a century ago and the sweat shop operators, more recently, who 'knew' what was best for the Negro. Your statement that 'congregation' rather than 'segregation' exists in Orange is reminiscent of those who have attempted to blind themselves to the problems of the Negro, thus creating further problems for the community…

We demand that you retract these unfounded statements as obviously a misunderstanding of actual conditions. We further demand that you, as one expressly stating a desire for the advancement of the City of Orange, resign your position in order to restore confidence among all the people in the community in our school board.

Doc, in a press statement, said:

Braun seeks to fool the federal government and the community when he arrogantly testifies that 90 percent of Negroes in Orange are satisfied with Jim Crow schools. His statement belies the fact that he and the Board of Education had several meetings which included the NAACP the Citizens for Representative Government, Central School PTA, Oakwood PTA, and Negro parents who were fighting to end segregation in the Orange schools.

Negroes in Orange, like Negroes everywhere, are opposed to segregation in every form. Therefore, I repeat that Braun should resign or be removed from the Board of Education for his complete lack of integrity.Braun's answer was, "No, I'm not going to resign. I don't have much time to read the newspapers... But from what I was told was in the newspapers, it's laughable... I don't run scared. I do what I think is right, what my conscience tells me. I can't be interested in whether Johnny Jones wants to go to another school because he doesn't like the other children he has to mingle with."

The city fathers had no power to remove Braun, since the board was an autonomous body. But CRG laid the groundwork to prevent his reappointment.

14 Walk In With Ben

THE FIRST MAYOR-COUNCIL election was set for May, 1963. Murphy was no longer acceptable to CRG and Alexander had long since decided not to run again. CRG set up a committee to recommend an alternate candidate. The popular choice was Colson Woody, a prominent businessman who had been appointed to the board of education in 1960. Woody was reluctant to run, so a Draft Woody movement was organized under the chairmanship of Benjamin F. Jones, who had recently become involved in CRG.

The committee met several times, but Woody either delayed his decision or declined. Finally, he said no.

"Well," Ben suggested to the committee, "how about Doc reconsidering?"

No, Doc definitely didn't want to run. "How about Preston?" Not him, either.

"Look, man, I'll tell you," Doc said, "we made a little decision. We picked our candidate. The fact is, we passed the hat and picked up enough money for a headquarters."

"Well, let me put my share in the hat – but who's the candidate?" asked Ben.

"You are, man," Doc announced. "Who'd you think?"

Ben Jones was a well-known figure around town, an ex-athlete, physical therapist, fraternity leader, life member of the NAACP, active in the YMCA.

Home first got to know Ben in the Harmony Bar, one of many favorite hangouts. Home talked politics, and Ben bought drinks all around. One day Ben got tired of being harangued. "Look," he said, "I work with the Y, NAACP, Community Chest, and my fraternity – isn't that enough for me to give to the community?" He threw some money on the bar and called to the bartender, "Set my man up with drinks. I'm leaving."

"Come back here," Home said sternly, "First of all, you don't walk out on Black folks like that, Ben. And second, I don't want your money or your drinks without you."

Ben apologized and stayed. That evening changed his life. On the eve of becoming a candidate, Ben had no clear idea of what politics and Black liberation were about. Moreover, there were problems in making him into a believable, hard-hitting candidate. In the beginning, he never came to headquarters without his "portfolio." Home used to say to him, "Man, that portfolio won't do you no good in the streets."

Benjamin F. Jones.

"But, Home," Ben would reply, "I got to carry my papers with me."

One evening, he accidentally left it at the headquarters. When he came in the next morning, it was not to be found. Seemed someone had thrown it in the trash can. Ben swore Home had done it. Home swore he hadn't, but Ben got the message and never brought the portfolio around again.

The committee members urged Ben to write a draft before his first public speech so they could point out the shortcomings when they reviewed it with him. It was loaded with four-syllable words. "Look," he was told, "we got to work on your speeches. You can't be going out in the street with all these big words."

Ben agreed to borrow a tape recorder to practice his speeches. When he later dropped his cards during a speech at Union Hall, he breezed through. Throughout the campaign, he was good-natured, quick to learn, and accepted criticism well. He soon became a real campaigner.

Ben was opposed by Pearl Overby and Bill Cook as well as Murphy, his main adversary. The white politicians put a white candidate in the race, calculating they might be able to steal the election if the Black vote were split.

Murphy figured to be out in front at the beginning of the race. He had run previously, he had an organization actively working for him, and he had support in the community. Ben had not been identified with running for office before, and CRG had to mobilize widely to garner votes for him.

The main strategy was to get out front and stay there, since CRG expected there would be a runoff. It was unlikely that any of the five candidates would receive a majority of the votes. CRG did not attack Murphy's group but tried to keep up the programmatic pressure, hoping Murphy would make mistakes. Home predicted that CRG's "superior forces, superior money, and superior know-how" would win.

Ben's campaign developed several advantages over Murphy's. The first was that Ben made limited coalition agreements with certain whites, including Nick Franco, who was running for mayor. Franco had his sign at Ben's headquarters and campaign workers canvassed for both candidates. This strengthened Ben's financial position since Franco paid for his share of the workers. It also meant that there would be a wider base for accomplishing programs the Black community needed if both Jones and Franco went into office. Altogether, CRG had fifty workers in the field to cover a ward of five districts. Each district was seven or eight square blocks, so they were well covered.

CRG workers were more seasoned in canvassing and getting out the vote than they had been in Alexander's campaign, and no longer relied on volunteers. They developed the practice of allocating sufficient funds to pay all workers for their election day work; each one was also required to canvass his area before election day.

This was a lesson Home had learned from the Hague machine. Hague depended on paid workers, using city employees to fill in the gaps. The amount of money involved is not large in comparison with the total cost of a campaign, but it buys accountability. Volunteers may or may not be reliable; paid workers have to be.

The campaign projected Ben as "a king-size man for a king-size job." Everyone was urged to "Walk right in with Ben," after a song popular at the time. The campaign took to the streets through door-to-door canvassers, street corner meetings, house parties, and bar parties. Women were again the backbone of the movement.

Ben led the election but polled less than 51 percent. Murphy was his opponent in the runoff, which took place a month later. CRG was able to win important support in the runoff for Ben from Pearl Overby and Bill Cook.

Victory depended on what the white voters who had voted for the white candidate would do now. Here CRG, through Home, Rudy Thomas, and others, had an advantage over

Murphy because they could reach for the support of organized labor. Again IUE Local 467 came into the fight with canvassers and other support. The Teamsters, UAW, and other unions also contributed. Murphy had no way to obtain labor backing, and this proved crucial to the outcome.

Home was able to get UAW support through Paul Krebs, who had been Joseph Minish's campaign manager when he ran for Congress; Home and Rudy had worked in Minish's campaign. Krebs sent ten UAW members to canvass where needed. They were experienced hands who knew what to look for and could bring in results.

Early in the runoff Preston called Home: "Look, Home, I was just invited to a meeting at Franco's, and I'm pretty sure it has something to do with the runoff. I think you better come along."

Franco was then head of the Orange Democratic Party. When they arrived at the meeting they found the ward leaders assembled. Someone said, "Hey, Mr. Grimsley." Then, noticing Home, "What's he doing here? This isn't an open meeting."

"Well," said Preston, "he's my adviser, and if you're going to talk about the campaign, I won't participate without him." Home stayed.

The meeting moved to the office of Jim Fittin, a leading Essex County Democrat. One of the ward leaders opened by suggesting that all Democrats in the city limit their efforts to Franco's runoff campaign and work only for him.

"Hold it right there," Home interrupted. "Franco hasn't won the election yet. If you try to pull this kind of move and take your forces out of Ben Jones's campaign, Franco will lose in our ward and will lose the election."

The argument continued for the rest of the meeting, with the party leaders eventually backing down a little. But a few days later a statement appeared in the paper that indicated they were still pursuing that policy.

Home got on the phone with Paul Krebs. "Look," he said, "these guys are trying to murder my candidate, and you better come in here and save them from themselves because if they keep this up, it will also end Franco's political career."

Krebs understood that this would make a shambles out of what was supposed to be a smoothly run campaign. Franco, by trying to pull workers out of Jones's campaign – workers that he did not control in the first place – would create disunity and bitterness and would lose support rather than gain it.

On the next Saturday that Congressman Minish was in town, a meeting was set up with Franco to settle the matter. Minish brought Franco to Ben's headquarters to verify the arrived-at understanding.

Meanwhile, rivalry in the ward between Ben and Murphy became intense. CRG had two sound trucks. One was sent to cover street meetings around the ward, while the other went to the Corner of Good Hope, where campaigning began every day early in the afternoon before Murphy's forces were available. With a variety of speakers and plenty of rock records, they could keep the meeting going for hours while Murphy's people stood around waiting to have the corner. CRG just kept going until it was too late for Murphy to hold a meeting.

Rebecca Doggett Andrade.

An incident happened which made Home again notice Rebecca Doggett. She came out of the Murphy headquarters over to where her workers were standing around, wasting time. "Come on," she told them, "don't just stand there. If we can't have this corner, let's go someplace else on the street. These old fools aren't going to let us have the corner if they can help it."

But the others didn't listen. The night before the election CRG had two meetings going and Murphy's camp had none.

Things were tight in the last days of the runoff. There was no more money to buy literature, and what was left had to be used in key areas. On the last day, Ben saw a man on a street corner with a car full of leaflets. He was talking over a sound system, "Vote for Ben Jones, walk in with Ben." Ben had never seen him before.

"Hey, man," Ben asked, "'where you from?"

"What business is that of yours?" came the reply.

"Well, I just wanted to know... "

"Can't you see I'm working?"

"Look, I'm Ben Jones, and I know we don't have any money to pay you or pay for these leaflets, so if you think you're going to get... "

"Listen, mister, I don't care who you are. Joey B. sent me. He told me 'Go out and campaign for Ben Jones.' So here I am."

Ben went back to headquarters, shaking his head. "Hey, Home, there's some guy down on the corner who says Joey B. sent him – who's Joey B.?"

"Joey B. is head of Teamster Local 97. I've worked with him over the years, so he said he would help us out in return."

Labor helped turn the tables, and Jones won the runoff. There was joy in the headquarters that night. The first Black representative had been elected to city government.

As the folks partied and congratulated themselves, a white Cadillac drove up full speed and screeched to a halt. Doc jumped out. "Hey, Ben," he called, "come here. The Man wants to see you. Dennis Carey is up at Franco's house and wants you."

"You mean it, Doc? I'll be with you in a minute."

"Ben," Home interjected, "don't you be going out of here tonight. If the Man wants to see you, he knows where you are. He spent this whole damn election trying to cut your throat, and now you're going to run off to him so he can. You just stay here with your people."

Ben stayed.

That night, Home went to the Murphy headquarters. He talked quietly with the campaign workers, urging them not to get discouraged and drop out of the fight. "You're young," he said, "and there are things you can do that some of us older people can't do any longer. We need your energy and your support in continuing the fight to bring a new day to Orange." Throughout his political life Home had been concerned with the development of young people and the building of bridges to make coalition politics possible. When he first began his involvement in Orange with the New Day campaign, he read this poem at a rally:[12]

> An old man going a lone highway,
> Came at the evening, cold and gray,
> To a chasm, vast and deep and wide,
> Through which was flowing a sullen tide.
> The old man crossed in the twilight dim,
> That sullen stream had no fears for him;
> But he turned, when he reached the other side,
> And built a bridge to span the tide.
>
> "Old man," said a fellow pilgrim near,
> "You are wasting your strength in building here.
> Your journey will end with the ending day:

You never again must pass this way.
You have crossed the chasm deep and wide;
Why build you the bridge at evening tide?"

The builder lifted his old gray head.
"Good friend, in the path I have come," he said,
"There followeth after me today
A youth whose feet must pass this way.
This chasm that has been naught to me
To that fair-haired youth may a pitfall be;
He, too, must cross in the twilight dim;
Good friend, I'm building this bridge for him."

That night, Home laid the foundation for future coalition with Becky Doggett and Eddie Andrade, who had also worked in Murphy's campaign. Over the years, they came to be among his closest friends and colleagues.

15 Home's Economic Policy in Orange

WITH BEN ON THE council, a new way of working became possible. Where previously CRG could only fight from the streets, now they could also fight from inside the council. The community's voice could be heard in chambers as well as on the floor at open meetings.

Ben met regularly with key CRG people. They devised a plan to make sure there were representatives of the Black community in all important areas of government.

In line with the NNLC contention that economics is the key to Black oppression, Home urged that they continue to fight for a piece of the economic pie in Orange.

As early as 1959, they sought to organize a company that would provide housing for families displaced by the Freeway. After Ben's election, the Freeway Development Corporation (FDC) was formed. The idea was to buy land and build houses. The city had empty lots, which the corporation, made up of CRG members and supporters, decided to bid for at assessed valuation. They went before the council and were turned down. Immediately they organized a campaign charging that the property had been denied to them because most of the stockholders were Black. FDC attorney Morton Stavis began negotiations with the city attorney and between them they worked out an approach.

But, when it began to look as if FDC would be able to buy some land, a rich out-of-town developer bid against them. The price was run up out of FDC's range, and the biggest lot was lost. FDC acquired several lots, but not enough to make a dent in the housing needs of the poverty area. As a result, no government money was available to develop the land, and FDC was stymied.

As part of the effort to have an impact on job discrimination in the construction industry in the city, a pre-apprenticeship training pilot project was set up in 1964.

The policy of exclusion of Blacks from the building trades and building trades unions began with apprenticeships, since that was where most of the skilled workers received their training and where the line of discrimination was most clearly drawn. According to the 1963 report of the N. J. Advisory Committee to the United States Commission on Civil Rights,

> ... there are only 14 Negro apprentices out of approximately 3,900 in the State of New Jersey attest(ing) to exclusion of Negroes from the program. The two dominant reasons emerge from lack of information among Negroes about the apprenticeship program and lack of enforcement of the existing non-discrimination clauses.

CRG felt that with combined city and state pressure, there was a chance to enforce the non-discrimination clause in the contract of the Washington-Dodd Urban Renewal Project.

Taking a chapter from the NNLC's Gateway campaign in Louisville, they established a training program based on the assumption that one of the major bases for exclusion was that many young Blacks could not pass the entrance examinations. They set up a committee of teachers and journeymen to instruct in shop mathematics and job familiarity. Ben Jones and Friendship House sponsored the program.

Ben asked his friend, Alan Sagner, president of Levin-Sagner Homes, builders of the project, for his cooperation. Sagner readily agreed to help. He also pledged to arrange meetings with the leadership of all the craft unions.

Sagner arranged separate meetings, at which Ben and Home were present, with representatives of each union involved in the project. He told them that if all the trades did not integrate, he would close down the job on grounds of breach of contract, without waiting for the government to move in. The unions were impressed. They moved. For the first time, there was a highly representative job situation in Orange construction.

In the meantime, CRG had begun its training program. At the first class, there were twenty students between the ages of sixteen and forty-three, most between eighteen and twenty-two. Slightly over half were unemployed, with the rest doing janitorial jobs, dishwashing, and truck driving. Many had deficiencies in simple math and English that would have kept them out of apprenticeships. The course lasted a month, two evenings a week, and the students were given proficiency tests. In addition, there were lectures on adjusting to a job situation.

The program was successful for the young men who participated, and it helped to desegregate the unions.

PHOTO GALLERY

Ernie at 19.

Executive Board Hudson County CIO Council; Ernie is in the first row, far right.

Young Ernie Thompson and Coleman Young at the National Negro Labor Council Founding Convention.

Ernie and Maggie get married.

Ernie with President Fitzgerald at UE Women's Conference. UE Archive.

At the Women's Conference, UE women signed a Proclamation supporting the Montgomery Bus Boycott. Rosa Parks sent a thank you letter, which is in Ernie Thompson's Archive at Rutgers University. UE Archive.

In this UE strike, women's equality is front and center of the union's demands. UE Archive.

Ernie with his son, Joshua Paul.

Maggie at Ben's campaign headquarters. Photo by Herb Way.

At the NNLC Reunion. Back row: Leibel Bergman and Maggie Thompson. Front row: Coleman Young and Ernest Thompson.

Ben Jones playing on new bocce courts, as the city celebrated the opening of a renovated park. Photo by Herb Way.

John Alexander was the special guest speaker at the opening of the new high school. Photo by Herb Way.

III. THE RIGHT TO LIVE AND WORK

*In the schools, the future of our children is being decided – who will live and who will die. We must make this the central programmatic issue of our struggle here in Orange: that **all** children shall have the right to live and work in this society.*

Ernest Thompson

16 Doc Becomes an Educator

Shortly after Ben's election, CRG turned again to the schools. Colson Woody was the only board of education member who had children in the system. The board's refusal to deal with segregation and overcrowding led CRG to demand that the entire board resign. Soon afterwards, Woody resigned in disgust, and asked the other members to follow suit.

Woody's unexpired term was open to another Black person. CRG thought it should be someone who would have the strength to lead the fight for real educational improvement. They agreed on Doc, the most outspoken critic in the city. To avoid appointing him, though, Mayor Franco approached various other Blacks.

CRG discussed how to deal with the situation. How could they make Franco appoint Doc and not somebody else?

"Let me tell you a little story," Home said. "When our union established a Fair Practices Committee, it wanted some Black person to head it. Our Black caucus decided I would be the best one for the job. I had had more experience in the union, I knew it better than anybody else, and I was a rough fighter. Plus, I had twenty years of seniority, and I could tell anybody 'go to hell, I'm going back into the plant.'

"So we combed the country, going to every potential Black candidate for the job – Joe Squires, Bill Smith, Sterling Neal – and making sure that Blacks who might be considered would not accept. See that? Would *not* accept. The officer in charge of hiring held out for a while, but finally he called Jim McLeish, who was chairman of the national Fair Practices Committee, and said, 'Send that Thompson over here. He's got the job.'

"Even if we couldn't decide who would get the job, we could decide who *wouldn't*. I think that's what we have to do in this situation. We'll go to the Blacks who might be considered, and we'll ask them to turn Franco down so that Doc, who's the most powerful representative the community could have, can get the job."

Everyone agreed. They went after the various people involved and were able to convince them that it would be best for Alexander to take the post. At the same time, Ben Jones kept the pressure on Franco. Doc was finally appointed in January 1964.

By that time, there was only a month and a half left before the state deadline for presenting a desegregation plan for Oakwood. Despite the pending loss of a quarter of a million dollars, the board had done nothing. It hoped to beat the ruling in the courts.

When Doc went on the board, he immediately offered a desegregation plan which was a modified version of the Princeton Plan, combining three school districts and sending all their sixth grades to Oakwood. The board deferred action since it was faced with another crisis – under the law, it had to reorganize by February 1. The president, William Braun, had not been reappointed, and none of the white members left was willing to step into the crossfire between the state and the community. On the one hand, if the board continued legal action, the city would lose state aid; on the other, if the board desegregated Oakwood, there would be stiff opposition from hostile whites.

As a way out, they offered the presidency to Doc. CRG felt that he could accept only if the board would agree to his desegregation plan. The board had no viable alternative. Doc became president. The Alexander Plan was adopted and submitted to the state board of education.

A weaker man or one without a firm community base could not have withstood the fury let loose at that point. Some of the parents of sixth-graders boycotted the Oakwood School. They called Alexander every name in the book, and even sought to win support from the Black community for their blatantly anti-Black activities. They agitated for "neighborhood schools" and agonized over the dangers to their children from the "long" walk to Oakwood. One of their tactics was to put out leaflets like the one entitled "Alexander's Ragtime School Plan," which they were afraid to sign.

They called Doc's home continually, vilifying him in private as they did in public, and they picketed his house, hoping he would break under the pressure.

CRG held a meeting to discuss what to do about the pickets. Since this was a case of whites straying into the ghetto, some of the folks on the corner were ready to "take care of business." But that would have resulted in citywide reprisals, and the Black community had no desire to take on the whole city.

Finally, Doc and his wife Emmy Lou came up with an idea: They made pots of coffee and served it to the picketers, pulling the teeth of their protest.

With the opening of the school year, some parents put their children into so-called "freedom schools" in homes and churches. A few Blacks went along with this, including Ray Murphy and the NAACP. But gradually the rebellion began to wither away. Alexander threatened to send parents to jail if they continued to break the law by keeping children out of

ALEXANDER'S RAGTIME ** SCHOOL PLAN

MAYOR-NIKITA-HITLER-DICTATOR-FRANCO
SAID I AM PROUD THAT I APPOINTED JOHN
(THE MURDERER) ALEXANDER TO THE BOARD
OF EDUCATION SO WE COULD DO THE FOLLOWING:

* WE WANT TO MURDER YOUR CHILDREN.

* WE DEMAND YOUR CHILDREN TO WALK INTO
  UNPROTECTED AREAS WHERE TRAFFIC IS
  EXTREMELY HEAVY.

* WE WANT YOUR CHILDREN TO WALK AT LEAST
  A MILE EACH DAY.

* LET'S REMEMBER PEARL HARBOR, WE LOST
  OUR BELOVED ONES WITH BULLETS--------
  AND NOW IT WILL BE WITH AUTOMOBILES!

MAYOR FRANCO ARE THERE ANYMOREALEXANDERS
(NOT THE COCKTAIL DRINK) IN YOUR CLOSET?

A RECALL IS A MUST

school, and that finished the protest. The Alexander Plan was ineffective in the end because many white parents sent their children to parochial or private school rather than have them in school with Black children. Out of an anticipated fifty-five white children, only twenty-one actually went to Oakwood.

Several years later, in a speech at Harvard University on the topic, "Is Quality Education Integrated Education?" Doc said:

> The conclusion that only integrated education is quality education deals a death blow to all Black ghetto children. By virtue of the physical impossibility and the violent anti-Negro attitudes and resistance of the whites in the inner city, integration is a hoax for the foreseeable future. The rapid exodus of middle class whites into the suburbs and the transfer of those remaining from public to private or parochial schools removes integration from any practical discussion as a legitimate solution to quality education for all.

CRG began to look in other directions for answers to Orange's educational problems.

17   Twenty Years of Neglect

AFTER DOC HAD BEEN on the board for a few months, it came time to prepare the budget for the next year. As they went from item to item, board members simply asked what had been allocated the year before so they could request the same amount again. A few times the secretary asked for money for maintenance, which was his special concern, and it was immediately written in. But every time the superintendent asked for changes or additions to educational programs, someone would object, "Is that really necessary? We have to keep the interests of the taxpayer in mind…"

There was no outlook of evaluation, revision, modernization, or expansion of the program. The school budget was 30 percent of the municipal budget, compared with 50 to 60 percent in neighboring communities. But the only problems which concerned the board members were how many new teachers they *had* to have and how they could avoid salary increases.

Around the same time, Doc learned that 43 percent of Orange's children were failing at least one subject by the time they reached the eleventh grade. He was shocked. He obtained the results of the California Test of Mental Maturity, a reading test, which revealed that 57 percent of the children in grades three through eight were below grade level and 58 percent were reading below their *own* level of expectancy.

The curriculum was totally inadequate: There was no language arts program, no real science program in the elementary grades, little use of modern math, a "manual arts" program which consisted only of making simple wooden articles, and music and art programs which were essentially baby-sitting classes. There was overcrowding in all schools and a high dropout rate.

Yet there was no parent or community involvement. The board had carefully ensured this through its procedures for public meetings. All the board's business – which could drag on for hours – was conducted first and all issues of importance were voted on. Only then was the meeting opened for public discussion. Controversial issues were taken up at closed meetings.

Neglect of education went back nearly a century, to 1869, when out of 2,000 children of school age, only 250 were attending school. In that year, a board of education was established, and the first school was built. Called a high school but serving all grades, it was on Day Street near Main, a building that later became City Hall. When it opened, there were thirty-seven pupils in the high school and 499 in the lower grades.

It was not until passage of the Compulsory Education Act of 1905 that large numbers began to attend high school. Pressures were great for young people to go to work to help support their families, but the high school emphasized classical training and had no orientation toward preparing those who would immediately enter the world of work. Out of a population of 25,000 in 1906, Orange had a high school graduating class of only thirty-two.

Even so, a larger building was needed, and Colgate High was constructed that year. When it became inadequate, a third high school was built in 1925. But the traditional emphasis on classical training and penny-pinching continued. The board of education was dominated by the same men who controlled the city. The outlook was to give as little as possible to public education; their own children were in private schools, so what did it really matter?

Sitting alone on the board, faced with these problems, Alexander was sick at heart.

"Home," he pleaded, "what are we going to do about this?"

Ernie had never worked on educational problems before; he had as much to learn as Doc. For a labor organizer to become an expert on education was a herculean task, but there were too many demands on Doc, so Home undertook to learn what he could. He finally concluded, "Doc, we must mobilize what resources we have. This school system is frozen in its tracks, and change will not come from within."

18   Community Help for Learning

IMMEDIATE RELIEF to the learning problems was organized by the community.

In the fall of 1964, the first Study Help program was begun at Oakwood for grades one through six. It was a tutoring program held four afternoons a week under the direction of Jo MacFarlane, a teacher, utilizing a staff of high school students. Study Help provided a place where students could do their homework and find assistance if they needed it. There were pens, pencils, paper, a quiet place to work, and encouragement. It was a tutoring center, rather than the limited one-to-one type of tutoring, making help always available to any student.

The next year, the Study Help program was funded by anti-poverty money and headed by Charles Simmons, another teacher. Students from the high school were again tutors. An unexpected bonus was that the high school students improved their own skills while helping the younger children.

An evening tutorial project for high school students was begun in February 1965. Called the Higher Achievement Tutoring Program, it was sponsored by the anti-poverty agency and the Lutheran Churches of America, through Upsala College. The program had been conceived as a one-to-one experiment, but the response was so overwhelming as to make that impossible. Five hundred students of a high school population of 1,000 took part voluntarily. It was pointed out in the project's report to the board of education:

> One of the most significant aspects of the program was that
> a tutorial program designed to aid the few was transformed
> into an educational system to help the many. We believe
> we have proof through the experience of this program that
> the tutorial system is available for mass help, with important
> new promise for deprived areas, and especially for the Negro
> ghetto, and that a one-to-one system is not necessarily the
> ideal tutorial situation.

The students were hungry for help when it was offered to
them in a dignified and concerned way. Youngsters who were
failing began to raise their grades to Bs and Cs and take an
interest in school.

But Ernie and others who watched the program unfold
heard the tutors muttering, "How can he learn when he can't
comprehend what he's reading? He doesn't even know the
alphabet." "How can he write when he can't spell?" "This child
doesn't know his times tables..."

The most common weakness was in basic language arts –
reading, writing, listening, and speaking. "It seems to me that
language arts are the key to learning," Home said to Doc.
"Without these tools, a child can't learn anything else. We've
seen the reading scores and the failure rates and how they go
hand in hand.

"If these children are denied the education they need to
participate in this technological society, what will happen to
them? I think this society has adopted a policy of writing off
poor children, Black and white, and is denying them a place.
They are being condemned to the scrapheap before they even
have a chance.

"In the schools, the future of our children is being decided – who will live and who will die. We must make this the central programmatic issue of our struggle here in Orange: that *all* children shall have the right to live and work in this society."

19   More on the Board

FIGHTING FOR CONTROL of the board of education became the means of carrying out this commitment. CRG did not fight for Black control – they fought for *coalition* control, a coalition dedicated to educating all children.

Doc had hoped when he went on the board that his presence there would speed the resignation of the other members. It did. As vacancies occurred, CRG had a say in replacements.

Franco suggested to Ben that Tom Kelly be put on the board. CRG knew Tom through his help with Friendship House, and they had heard that he could be trusted. Franco liked him because he worked for Murray and Murray, an established law firm whose younger partner was then city attorney. Franco envisioned Kelly's appointment to the board as a counter-balance to Alexander.

Murray and others warned Tom to "Watch out for that Alexander. He's always around stirring up trouble. First with the integration business. Now he wants to shake up the whole school system. He's bossy and arrogant – a real radical."

For the first weeks, Kelly avoided Doc. But soon he could see that he was the one who had ideas as to how to improve the educational system. One evening, Doc called Tom aside after a meeting and said, "You got a minute, Tom? I want to talk to you about a few things. I wanted to tell you some of the things I've been trying to do on the board so maybe you can take a hand."

Tom agreed, and they began to develop a coalition. When Mrs. Murray left the board, CRG opened discussions with Franco about appointing a Black woman. "I can see why you want somebody Black," said Franco, "but why a woman?"

They explained to the mayor that women deserved to be in government as much as men, and that Black women were the most unrepresented group of all. As mothers and taxpayers, their stake in education was as great as that of anyone else. Franco finally agreed, and CRG offered him two names. He chose Hazel Rollins, a Rutgers Law School student and the wife of a leading local surgeon.

Hazel Rollins.

Daniel DiVincentis joined the coalition, and within a year there was a whole new outlook on the board. With these votes, rapid progress was possible. They first sought to establish a new relationship with the teachers. Orange for years had suffered from a higher than usual share of incompetent teachers and those rejected by other systems. It had a high turnover of teachers leaving for higher-paying jobs. All this resulted from a salary scale which was the lowest in Essex County.

Home emphasized to Doc, "Workers have a right to fair wages, decent treatment, and grievance procedures. I will not support you if you clash with the unions." The board equalized salary inequities and set up grievance procedures to foster a closer working relationship with the teachers.

After years of neglect of the educational system, many teachers tended to cling to obsolete methods and resist innovation. Many had not been back to school since they graduated. To correct this, Alexander created pay compensation and other incentives for resumption of study. But the measures took effect slowly. Some preferred a lower salary to continued training. The board accordingly had to provide extensive in-service training to ensure that teachers would learn to use new materials being introduced.

The community was involved. Board meetings were opened to the public and advisory committees were set up. The school facilities committee, one of the first, was headed by Rebecca Kingslow, an active member of CRG. Their job was to plan for the building and educational needs of the system. Their work revealed another aspect of the twenty years of neglect. Letters from the Middle States Association of Schools and Colleges and from the state and county boards of education came to light. These were the bodies responsible for accreditation. As far back as 1935, they had criticized the high school for overcrowding and failure to serve the needs of the majority of the students.

Rebecca Kingslow.

Year after year, the letters had continued to come. With Doc on the board, the city had its first chance to find out what was going on. And it was almost too late. In 1964, the County

129

Department of Education had said:

> We have very serious reservations about the adequacy of
> the high school plant. In our opinion it is not possible
> to operate an effective broad program such as is needed
> in Orange today in the present building. The following
> conditions are cited:
>
> ... there are too few classrooms to permit the reduction
> in the size of large classes because the school is already
> being used beyond its functional capacity;
>
> there are no remedial classes;
>
> the library is about half the size it should be;
>
> the art room is totally inadequate;
>
> the same may be said of the clothing room; the metal
> shop and the wood shop are both incapable of handling
> more than a small minority of the students who could
> benefit from such experience.

When Doc found this out, he immediately moved to call
in the state Department of Education for an evaluation. Their
report said:

> ... the Orange Senior High School building is a sound,
> and well-maintained, physical structure that can certainly
> serve an important purpose in the district's housing
> program. But certainly, were all the desirable areas
> provided within this building for the secondary level, the
> probable functional capacity of this building would be
> substantially less than 500 pupils.

The school facilities committee recommended, and the board agreed, that Orange would have to build a new high school to meet the needs of the students.

During this period, the board had been trying to define what it meant by "educational needs." The children it was educating would enter a highly technological society, with fewer and fewer jobs for untrained hands. Workers would need a strong foundation in basic skills – language arts, math, and science – and competence within a range of occupations, so that they could be trained and re-trained as the job market changed. For 80 percent of the youngsters, their education ended with Orange High. The obsolete wood, metal, and clothing classes were not sufficient to prepare these 80 percent for participation in the *world of work*.

The high school tended to discriminate against those who would go to work immediately. The best teachers and materials were reserved for the college bound. Those who sought technical training, or were behind in reading and other skills, got the crumbs. Vocational teachers were considered a step below academic teachers.

Recognizing this, the board moved toward a concept of education which involved the best and newest ideas for teaching all children – an education to prepare the college bound *and* the vocational-technical student with a creative interdependence of academic and technical learning. In seeking to express its commitment to this kind of "comprehensive" education, the board for the first time adopted a philosophy of education.

It opened with the words, "We believe in the worth and dignity of every individual."

20   A Second Chance

In 1965, the State of New Jersey announced that Title I money – aid to education for disadvantaged children under the Elementary and Secondary Education Act – was available to school systems. Local groups were given two weeks to program use of the funds. CRG moved quickly to earmark the money to meet the needs of Orange's children.

An immediate practical question was how to get someone on the program committee. Alexander, by a careful reading of the law, found that the community was entitled to a representative through the anti-poverty agency, Orange Opportunity Corporation (OOC). Home, who was chairman of the OOC education committee, was certified as community representative on the Title I committee. Doc also made sure that the Catholic educators were represented.

In preliminary discussions at CRG, it was decided that language arts should be the core of the Title I program and that it should concentrate on grades kindergarten through sixth, the crucial years in language arts training. Anti-poverty moneys could then be concentrated on the upper grades.

Culture was deemed the second key aspect of the program. Poor children and Black children didn't know their history and culture. It was important for them to learn about their own art, dance, theatre, literature, and music, as well as that of others.

The third aspect was medical care. Some of the children had

never had a physical examination; many had health problems or vision or hearing defects that could contribute to learning deficiencies.

With this understanding, Home went to the first Title I meeting. Doc was there to back him up. Home faced a roomful of professional educators. Dr. Leonard Cronk, superintendent, went from person to person, polling them for program ideas. They had little to offer. Finally, he reached Home, who began, "I think we should have a program centered around language arts, with a strong emphasis on cultural arts and medical care."

"But," said one educator, with a patronizing smile, "we have a language arts program."

"You have no language arts program worthy of the name," Home replied.

Doc said later he thought the educator would faint as she stared at the unlettered Homeboy.

Some of the Catholic educators present came forward to support Home, but by then he had the offensive. By the end of the meeting, the only concessions he had made were to Dr. Crank's proposal of a name, "Operation Development of the Whole Child," and his suggestion for a summer camping program.

Once Home had succeeded in blasting through the establishment red tape at the first meeting, others began to speak out, too.

Having reached agreement on the kind of program, CRG then fought for allocation of funds in the priorities agreed on. An important victory was the earmarking of $32,000 for teacher aides. These were to be community people who would work as part of teaching teams in the primary grades. By providing personal attention to individual children, they would free teachers to work with the entire class. It was also hoped

Orange's Title I children.

that this would lead to a closer relationship between schools and parents.

Some of the professionals were incensed at money being used for non-professional personnel. They refused to admit that community people had a contribution to make to education. But CRG held its ground and finally won.

Because of the vast need for improvement in the Orange schools, the Title I program was conceived as being a *proving ground* for ideas and techniques that offered the most help to deprived children. Innovations were tried in Title I classrooms, including the Peabody language arts manuals and i.t.a., a system of reading and writing based on a phonemic alphabet. As new methods proved successful, they were introduced into the whole school system.

Ceramics, photography, sewing, metal and plastics technology, dance, and camping were added to the curriculum for the sake of the "whole child."

Orange Title I from its inception was one of the outstanding programs in the country. It was a success for all the children in the city because the degree of educational improvement at the lowest level placed greater demands on educational programs at all levels.

When the children came to their Title I classrooms, they became quiet and orderly, eager to follow instructions. Sometimes within two weeks, "uneducable" children were reading and writing. Title I teachers believed in their pupils and gave them the extra attention they needed; regular teachers were forced to respect the changes they saw in the children.

The children continued to accomplish and grow. In their words, "we created stories," "we wrote and acted plays," "we read a newspaper," and "we learned to use a movie camera, develop and enlarge pictures."

Many parents were enthusiastic. They became involved in the program through meetings, participation on committees, work as volunteer or paid aides in classrooms, and open houses where the youngsters displayed their new skills and interests.

But it was difficult for some of the educators to change their attitudes. Home and Doc heard reports that some children who did not respond immediately were being sent to the school psychologist and labeled "emotionally disturbed." "Damn," said Home, "they found a new way to write off these little children."

No one could ignore the fact, however, that out of those preliminary discussions in the community, an exemplary program had been born – conceived not by the educators but in the hearts and minds of the people.

21   The Time Is Up

THE PROBLEM OF implementing new educational programs in overcrowded schools arose repeatedly. It became increasingly clear that the solution hinged on building a new high school.

To build a new school with adequate facilities would take more money than the board had, so the question would have to go to the council for bond approval. That meant taking it before the voters. How could they convince the voters to spend the money? And how would the decision be made as to what the voters' money was spent *for*?

Doc called Home one day. "Home, I got an interesting book I want you to look at."

It was a report of a conference at M.I.T. on the comprehensive high school. The conference was led by Dr. Nathaniel Frank, a world-renowned physicist who was concerned that the secondary schools were not preparing their students. He had called together a number of educators for six weeks of workshops, and they had put forward in educators' language many of the ideas Doc and Home had been pushing for in Orange.

The report stated that:

1. All youth should be prepared to enter the world of work.
2. Some of the skills and concepts in "vocational" education were needed by all children, at all educational levels.

3. Education should be a continuing process, going on throughout a person's life, and not terminal.

4. Vocational students needed to know more than one limited set of skills – they needed understanding and knowledge of how to work in a group of related fields; for example, girls in clothing would learn sewing, dress design, retailing, and other aspects of the field.

5. Vocational education should deal with all areas of learning skills – intellectual, manipulative, social, and creative.

6. Education in school could at best provide the basis for total vocational competence and make it easier for the individual to be trained on the job.

The conference proposed that all students be taught by doing as well as by the formal transfer of knowledge through the spoken and written word, knowing that, "I hear and I forget; I see and I remember; I do and I understand."

At Doc's invitation, Dr. Frank came to Orange to speak to teachers and interested citizens. He put his prestige behind the idea of a comprehensive high school for Orange. He also suggested that business and industry lend a hand to provide dramatic back-up on the need for comprehensive education.

A Labor-Business-Industry Committee was organized and held two conferences which Dr. Frank addressed. As long as Doc was on the board, the committee continued to play a role in developing the new high school along realistic lines, and was an additional channel for community involvement in education.

If the board wanted to win the struggle, they had to document to the satisfaction of the citizenry that the old high school was obsolete, that a new high school had to be built, and that it should in fact be a comprehensive high school rather than the old-model track system. As part of the campaign, Dr. Ronald

Doll from Columbia University made a cursory report in the spring of 1965. Then Rutgers University was hired to make an in-depth study of the existing facilities and their limitations, including plant, curriculum, and faculty.

In 1966 the Middle States Association found the high school so inadequate that it extended accreditation only on a limited basis for one year. On November 23, 1966, the board voted that "the City of Orange needs a new comprehensive high school" and called for the allotment of $4.4 million, based on figures prepared by the Educational Development Association.

The proposal then went to the Board of School Estimate for approval. But there were not enough votes to pass it.

The city was faced with a crisis. Its high school was inadequate for 80 percent of its students, and it was about to lose its accreditation. But Orange had to be convinced that it faced such a crisis. CRG evolved a strategy of mobilizing popular pressure and winning votes on the Board of School Estimate and the city council.

The board played its part by sending out a pamphlet called "Orange's Urgent Educational Needs" to all taxpayers. It reprinted copies of the letters condemning the high school and pointed out that the city had no other choice. It traced the historical roots of the problem: Forty years before, when the high school was built, one wing had been omitted for the sake of economy, dooming the building to inadequacy from the beginning.

"Let's not economize with our children's future," the pamphlet urged. Recognizing that cost was a big factor, the board called in Milton A. Zisman, a CPA, and gave him the task of finding out what the high school would actually cost the taxpayers after all available state aid had been applied. They also asked him to look into a feasible method of financing.

The next phase was to build a coalition, Black and white, committed to quality education for all children. The future of all the children of Orange was at stake in this fight. It would take the broadest possible mobilization to do battle for them.

22   Walk On With Ben

BEN WAS UP FOR re-election in 1967. His first four years in office had been a process of learning while doing. He had had no time for mistakes or beginner's luck. Nevertheless, he began to gain polish and confidence.

He was limited in what he could do by bad government. Many of the officeholders were holdovers from the days of commission government, and their attitudes reflected this. The city refused to hire a business administrator, the majority on the council preferring to have business matters be as decentralized as possible. Opportunities for coalition were limited by the caliber of the councilmen.

Ben was able to get his program together and work on issues that interested him. Principal among them was Friendship House, the only year-round recreational facility in the ward. It was housed in a run-down building and had uncertain funding and limited programs. The dedication of its employees, Gladys Taylor and Jesse Miles, was what made it notable. Year after year, Miles turned out great basketball players; all he needed was a court and some balls. Ben wanted to make Friendship House a frontline community center servicing a variety of needs and ages.

It developed that Friendship House was about to be destroyed. It was in the path of the Freeway that was coming through. Whatever funds were received from the sale probably would not be enough to relocate and rebuild. Ben hoped to convince the state that the center had "intrinsic value" in its meaning to the neighborhood, making it worth more than its paper value. Once he received the money, he had to keep the city fathers from using it for other purposes. The council at length agreed to put the funds in escrow while additional moneys for rebuilding were sought.

The second problem was an operating budget. Historically, under the commission system, funds for Friendship House had been part of the general allotment of the Department of Parks and Public Property. Ben worked it out so that Friendship House was given a line item in the budget so that there would be no danger of its being cut out altogether.

Of more importance, however, was his move to incorporate the center. It was decided that part of the funding would have to come from foundations, which would not give grants to a city-controlled organization. Tom Kelly then became the attorney for Friendship House and worked out arrangements to put it under the control of a board of trustees. The city's interest was preserved by having elected officials on the board. Ben worked on various other projects, including Freeway Development Corporation and other housing problems, educational problems, and the expansion of recreation. His careful work laid the basis for achieving much of the New Day program. But the work was far from finished. When election time rolled around again, CRG called on the voters to *Walk On With Ben*.

CRG sought to influence the city in favor of the new high school. While continuing to work on existing programs, such as tutorial and Title I, they moved out into the campaign.

One of CRG's efforts over the years had been to reach out to and organize Black people in various parts of the city. They had formed the South Ward, North Ward, and West Ward Organizations for Good Government, which were brought together with CRG into an umbrella organization called the Amalgamated Organizations for Good Government, enabling Blacks to have a citywide impact on Orange politics.

Now the Amalgamated Organizations needed to line up votes for the $4.4 million bond issue for the high school, which would have to pass first in the Board of School Estimate and then in the council. There had to be other favorable votes on the council besides Ben's.

But a new political situation was shaping up citywide: 1967 was the year of the "hot summer." Reactionary leaders in the white communities sought to base themselves on fear and racism, to fan the flames of racial discontent, and to organize what they called the "white backlash" to make sure Blacks did not win their objectives.

One day, Franco called in some of the CRG leaders and announced, "I've decided to go with the backlash. My opponent, John Monica, is pushing backlash, and if I'm associated with Jones and his policies, I'll never make it."

This left CRG with a problem. The coalition on which they had worked since the first Alexander campaign in 1958 was breaking up. After all his years in office, Franco was going to try to fool the white voters about where he was coming from. Whatever happened to him, CRG still had to find ways to proceed.

The Amalgamated Organizations had a conference to decide election policy, and Franco was invited to attend. When he didn't show up, the question came up whether to support him.

Home explained the new situation, "We don't want to get all tied up in the mayoralty question, but at the same time we don't want to attack Franco. That would drive him further into the arms of the whites in favor of backlash and aid his policy of deserting us. I think we should say, 'a plague on both your houses,' and boycott the majority line until the runoff.

"But there are still some whites who were on the council and have not deserted our coalition. There's Vincent DeRosa, Harry Callaghan, and Carmine Capone. We can continue to support them."

There was consensus. They also agreed that in the runoff, the campaign committee – which represented all the Amalgamated Organizations – would make policy based on the evolving situation.

John F. Kennedy.

For the next step in the school fight, it was important to deny votes to those whites who did not support the new high school and to promote other whites who did. Amalgamated agreed to support Capone in the North Ward; Quincy Lucarello in the West Ward; Callaghan in the South Ward; and Vincent DeRosa at-large. All of these candidates had agreed to a limited coalition with Ben.

CRG got busy in the East Ward. Charles Simmons, John Cosby, Bill Cook, and a white candidate named Conrad Marzano were running against Ben this time. Home brought up the problem of strategy for the ward. He told the leadership, "It's likely this white candidate will make it into the runoff. Therefore, we have to avoid attacking the Blacks in the race. We've got to make sure that there's nothing they can say against Ben when the time comes for them to support him in the runoff."

"We can base our campaign on Ben's achievements in office,"

said John Kennedy, the campaign manager. "But what if the white goes into the runoff?"

"Well, I think then we'll have to adopt a two-pronged attack, ward and race, that the ward deserves representation and that the reason this cat is out there in the first place is to cut Ben," replied Home.

There was unanimous agreement.

CRG went around the ward proclaiming Ben's record. Franco set out to harass the campaign by sending cops to arrest Home and others for using the sound truck "without a permit." It happened first at the Corner of Good Hope, where Becky Doggett Andrade was speaking: "Walk on with Ben Jones. He has proven himself…" Several police cars drove up. Ben went over to them.

"I'm sorry, Councilman, but I'm afraid we have to ask you to stop."

"Well, I don't see why," he replied. "We're not going to stop. These people are here at my request and they will not leave except at my request. If you want to arrest my friends, you'll have to arrest me, too."

"No, we weren't told to arrest you, Councilman. But you don't have a permit, so you have to stop."

"We don't have a permit and I've never seen a permit, and we will not stop."

Becky kept talking, "Ben led the way…"

Finally, the police, unwilling to arrest Ben, left, and the meeting continued, longer than usual, as an answer to the harassment.

But Ben wasn't always around. One day, the police caught Home and Charles Millis on Park Avenue with the mobile unit and arrested them. Ben got a call to come to the jail. "Let me find out what's happening," he started, but Home yelled, "See what's happening, hell! I want out."

Ben talked to the officers in charge and got Millis and Home released in his custody. The matter went to court, where they were found guilty. They obtained a lawyer from the ACLU, Arthur D'Italia, and appealed. The decision was reversed, and the ordinance invalidated. The sound trucks moved again.

It was a good, smooth campaign, better managed on every level than the first one had been. One funny but significant incident occurred at a fundraising barbecue. Ben ordered the food and let himself be talked into London broil instead of ribs because it would be easier to serve and was "tasty." When Home heard that, he blew up.

"Ben, don't you have any respect for people's culture and dignity? How could you even think of having a barbecue for Black folks and serving London broil? Home folks never even heard of London broil!" He was so furious that Ben went right out and bought some ribs.

When the vote came in, Ben led but, as predicted, the white candidate went into the runoff against him. As people gathered in the headquarters, Home and Preston Grimsley went off to hunt down the other Black candidates and bring them in so that people could hear them come out in support of Ben. Later, Home and other CRG leaders went to visit each of the candidates. "We know you support Jones," they said, "so we'd like to ask you to canvass and put out your sound truck, or give us some people." If they refused, Home could then go out and tell people in the streets they must be supporting the white candidate.

The candidates balked, but the pressure from all over the ward to have a Black representative made it impossible for them to hold out. They might have wanted to support the white candidate, but it would have meant the end of them politically.

The problem of what to do about Franco came up again, and CRG went to see him. They told him they would support him in the runoff if he promised to reappoint Doc to the board of education if he was re-elected. They also asked him to reappoint Tom Kelly to the board. Tom had proven to be a staunch friend, even declining a proffered partnership in his firm which was conditioned on his disassociating himself from Alexander and the CRG.

"Well, I'll reappoint Alexander," said Franco. "But I don't know about Kelly. I won't give you any promises on Kelly right now."

"O.K., that'll do," CRG said. They went on discussing campaign strategy. They knew Kelly was safe because Franco had missed the deadline for appointing someone else, automatically putting him in for another year. They figured what Franco didn't know wouldn't hurt them.

Runoff time rolled around. Ben won in the East Ward. Monica defeated Franco – the backlash didn't trust him after all, and he was not able to pick up the momentum he had lost in the first election. The coalition succeeded in electing Lucarello, Capone, and Vincent DeRosa.

Franco was so mad that he tried to appoint somebody else to replace Kelly on the board of education. But Tom took the matter to court and the appointment was knocked out.

Expectations were high that now there would be enough votes on the council to pass the bond issue for the new high school.

23   In the Streets

Before showdown time arrived, sufficient votes had been collected for the issue of the new high school to pass in the Board of School Estimate. The resolution went to the council, where it was hoped that the coalition of Jones, Brown, and Callaghan could pick up one more vote for a majority.

The racists began their campaign, claiming it was too much money for a school for "them." They were distorting the facts: The high school was 50 percent white.

CRG had to minimize errors – the stakes were too high – so they adopted a strategy of moving the coalition into the streets and forcing the state to keep pressure on the council.

On July 29, 1968, the resolution came before the council for the first time. The bigots out-organized the coalition, took the front seats, and dominated the meeting with cries that they would be bankrupted by the new school. Home and others spoke, but it was not enough. The resolution was defeated:

FOR	AGAINST
James Brown	Carmine Capone
Harry Callaghan	Vincent DeRosa
Ben Jones	Quincy Lucarello
	Richard Savage

Home entered the hospital for an operation but still directed a two-pronged attack from his bed. The Ad Hoc Committee for a New High School was formed on August 5, with Dr. Alexander and Robert Crowley, a white businessman and leader of the Junior Chamber of Commerce, as co-chairmen.

The committee sent a telegram to Governor Richard J. Hughes, State Education Commissioner Carl L. Marburger, and the state board of education:

> As a result of Orange City Council's action last Tuesday rejecting the proposed $4.2 million bond issue for expansion of high school facilities, a cross-section of the city decries this punitive action against the children of Orange. A committee of Black and white, business and professional, demand the State Department. of Education withdraw approval of Orange High School and $500,000 in State aid and administer the prerogative of making invalid the diplomas.

If the state would live up to its former threats, the council would have no recourse except to authorize the new school.

The council held a second meeting on August 6. Before it started, committee members picketed City Hall. They formed the nucleus of the crowd of 150 that filled the council chambers.

Dr. Alexander, speaking for the committee, said, "By your unfortunate action of last Tuesday, you have denied the children of Orange an adequate education. By your action, you have moved to damage their lives. You are only trustees of the assets of the community and, being trustees, you must act in the best interests of those whom you represent. You cannot take the cheapest way out."

Capone raised objections about which school buildings would be returned to the tax rolls. Hazel Rollins challenged this, saying, "To use this as an excuse is not acting in good faith.

The plan which evolved was a compromise. You all know that. If it was unacceptable, you should have said so then."

Students spoke, including Orange High Tornado basketball player Harvey Glover, who said a new school was needed to enable Orange's teams to be competitive with other schools.

Bernadine Oliver, a recent graduate who had been editor of the literary magazine, *Satori*, declared: "The real issue here is who is going to control the Black man's education. Black students have a harder time getting into college. I am going to college, and I am afraid that my background is limited. The children bused to Oakwood School were mostly Black. Their education is just as important as that of the whites."

When the vote was taken, it was three for and three against. Savage abstained.

Alexander called on those present to continue the protest until the next council meeting, two weeks hence.

On Saturday, August 10, young people held a rally on Main Street.

The next Monday, the committee sponsored a march by hundreds, Black and white, of all ages, including one woman who went the route in her wheelchair. Students led, chanting and singing.

Homes of opposing councilmen were picketed. The committee met with the board of education to urge them to hold firm.

On August 13, thirty-five members of the committee went to Trenton to meet with Dr. Joseph Clayton and Dr. William Warner of the Department of Education to press them to take action against the city if the new high school was defeated. The state officials led the discussion away from the urgent problem facing Orange.

Finally, Maggie Thompson said, "We're talking about

Design of proposed new high school prepared by architect Emil A. Schmid.

everything except what we came here to talk about. We're here to ask you to keep your promise to penalize the city if the council members refuse to build a new high school. The state has said over and over that the city must build the school. If you will just stand firm on that, if you will just tell the councilmen that they will lose state aid if they refuse to build that high school, then the children of Orange and the citizens of Orange will win."

The Department of Education eventually agreed to send the council a telegram to that effect.

The committee then met with Paul Ylivisaker, Commissioner of Community Affairs and New Jersey's outstanding official when it came to responding to urban problems. He agreed to help by finding $1 million in aid to construction costs to ease the financial burden on the city.

Organizations throughout the city began to come out in favor of the high school. The Orange Merchants' Association and the Chamber of Commerce both voted for it. When the Junior Chamber of Commerce refused to take the same stand, Robert Crowley resigned as vice-president.

Preachers preached and people marched as the final hour drew near.

The opposition was busy too. Anthony Imperiale of Newark, known for his clashes with Black activists, came to help his friends in the North Ward. "I'm going to be at the next council meeting," he announced.

The Ad Hoc Committee sent telegrams to the Attorney General and the Essex County prosecutor, requesting observers at the meeting.

Tension mounted. The weather was oppressively hot. Nerves were taut.

On the evening of August 19, committee members assembled and marched to Central school, where the meeting was to be held. Every seat in the auditorium was filled; scores who arrived late were turned away. There were 1,500 in the hall. Suddenly, the doors opened, and Imperiale marched in, followed by seventy-five men in their shirtsleeves who elbowed their way to the front and placed themselves at stage right. At stage left were the United Brothers, young Black militants, standing with crossed arms. In the center was the microphone. Behind it on the stage were the councilmen, seated around a long table. Throughout the hall were police with billy clubs, riot helmets, and mace cans. Television lights blazed, adding to the heat.

Council President DeRosa opened the meeting by saying, "I move we have the public hearing after we vote."

"What good will it do *after* we vote?" Ben challenged. The maneuver was defeated.

Capone immediately moved to introduce a resolution for $3 million for the high school, saying the state had promised to supply the rest. He also stated that he, Lucarello, DeRosa, and Mayor Monica had met with the state board of education in Trenton and that no punitive measures would be forthcoming for failure to approve the new building.

Ben crumpled a copy of the resolution and threw it over the side of the stage to Tom Kelly, who read it and shook his head vigorously.

Doc spoke first. "I challenge the legality of the motion that has just been presented to the council. Only the board of education can make the proposal for the new school, and the city must act on the board's recommendation. We have fooled around long enough. Give our children the high school they need!"

Michael O'Neil, a white executive who had functioned as a leader of the Labor-Business-Industry Committee in support of the new school, then spoke. "I'm addressing my remarks to those councilmen other than Jones, Brown, and Callaghan. I want *them* to hear me. Stop playing with education and let's get that new high school!"

The crowd roared approval and gave him a standing ovation. It was punctuated by catcalls from the opposition. Tom Kelly warned, "If this council tries to pass any illegal resolutions, I'll have you in court tomorrow."

"You're playing Russian roulette and the bullet is in the chamber tonight," Reverend Russell White told the council.

Student Harvey Glover asked the city fathers, "Why do you have to have so many policemen here? Why don't you just do right?"

Father Charles Brady declared, "You have a moral obligation to pass the new high school tonight."

As the speakers continued, the odor of tear gas suddenly filled

Dr. John Alexander addressing the meeting of the Orange City Council which authorized the new high school. Photo by Irving Overby.

the auditorium. A wave of panic swept the crowd, but discipline held and they remained in their seats.

It was finally proposed that the council vote. Capone pressed his motion, but Ben protested. "I'm not prepared to deal with anything that wasn't before the council prior to this evening. I know nothing of Councilman Capone's trip to Trenton. I know nothing about an ordinance that he wants voted on tonight. I do know that there is an ordinance before this council that *must* be voted on tonight. I propose that we end the public hearing at this time, that we recess for ten minutes, and that we come back and vote."

The councilmen filed off the stage. It was a tense ten minutes.

Offstage, Ben exhorted his colleagues, "We have to vote now. We have no other choice. We're under compulsion from the state, we've had in-depth studies, and this is what we have to do. We have to build that school. We have come to that agreement, except that some of us say it's too expensive. I submit that if we fail to pass the resolution tonight, it will be more expensive than any of us ever dreamed."

The council returned and the voting began.

"Councilman Brown?"

"Aye."

"Councilman Callaghan?"

"Aye."

"Councilman Capone?"

"Aye."

"Councilman DeRosa?"

"No!"

"Councilman Jones?"

"Aye."

"Councilman Lucarello?"

"Aye."

Savage's "Abstain" was lost in the joyous bedlam that broke loose. The people had won!

IV. HOMEBOY GOES TO NEWARK

For a more equal piece of the economic pie.

Ernest Thompson

24   Job Democracy

ORANGE'S PROXIMITY to Newark made for considerable social and political ties between the two Essex County cities and led to Ernie's involvement in Newark politics. In the 1950s, the Negro Labor Council led a struggle to break a gerrymander and win Black representation in the Central Ward. The election of Irvine Turner to the city council in 1954 opened the way for similar victories throughout the state. Ernie was deeply involved in those efforts.

He later participated in the Newark Coordinating Council (NCC) job struggles, the Committee for Negro Progress in 1966, Crusade for Learning, and Tri-City Citizens Union for Progress. His coworkers in Orange gave their backing to Ernie when he went to Newark and stood by if he needed support.

The struggles in Newark were bread-and-butter efforts involving diligent work day after day. Asked if he remembered any exciting stories of those days, he replied, "Nope, it was just hard work."

But the work had its rewards. Clarity of purpose and political actions based on well-defined issues characterized the campaigns, which included Black representation, the right to apprenticeships, coalition, education, and the dignity of Black culture.

He worked closely with Eddie and Becky Doggett Andrade, the young people he had met when they lived in Orange and worked with Murphy's organization. Although they found it hard at first to understand what Home was saying – he often spoke in his own kind of shorthand – they recognized his ability and soon became his students as well as his friends. Eddie often stopped by to tell Home about the projects he was involved in. One was a jobs fight led by the NCC at the Barringer High School site. NCC had attempted a head-on clash with the unions, which ended in bitter feelings on both sides. Home felt it had been a wrong tactic.

Edward Andrade.

He explained that segregation is a three-party conspiracy involving the contractors and the state, as well as the unions. While the union movement was strong enough to ignore pressure from a community group, government officials were open to political pressure.

Moreover, there were non-discrimination clauses in contracts, especially when state and federal moneys were involved. And the union did not have the sole right to place apprentices – the contractor could place 50 percent of them.

Two big construction jobs were coming up in Newark in the spring of 1964 – Rutgers Law School and Newark College of Engineering (NCE). Both were using state moneys and Urban Renewal lands; both would be using all-white construction crews.

NCC at that time included Newark Ministers for Progress, Americans for Democratic Action (ADA), the Congress of Racial Equality, the Negro–American Labor Council, and others. Eddie convinced NCC to undertake the jobs fight and to designate him as chief negotiator and Home as labor advisor.

They initiated an apprenticeship tutoring program at the Community Mobilization Center, a project co-sponsored by Essex ADA and the Urban League.

NCC then went to see Louis Danzig, director of the Newark Housing Authority, with the demand that he set up machinery to police the non-discrimination clause in the contract for purchase of the land. Under pressure, he finally agreed.

However, officials of Newark College of Engineering had to be convinced to talk; picketing was organized in May to bring them to the negotiating table. Early stages were directed towards getting them to accept the idea that Blacks and Puerto Ricans were entitled to a fair share of jobs and that they had a responsibility to enforce and police the anti-discrimination clauses in the contracts.

Rutgers in this respect was a lot more cooperative than NCE. Willard Heckel, dean of the law school, learned that he had to flex his muscles to even get a racial breakdown of workers on the job. After he threatened to close the job, a list was provided, and he was pleased that there were over 30 percent Blacks on it. But NCC quickly pointed out that they held only unskilled jobs – there were no minority journeymen or apprentices. Agreement on racial balance was reached with Rutgers in June, after one month of talks.

As a result of the talks, it was concluded that the ironworkers were key to job discrimination in the area; if they could be forced to hire minorities, the rest of the trades would follow.

When negotiations resumed in September, some improvements

had been made, particularly with the cement workers. But the plumbers tried to get around the demand by using Blacks only as laborers, and the ironworkers were circumventing it by not using any apprentices.

When NCC met again with Rutgers officials, they informed them that the candidates were ready and asked them to push the ironworkers to set up a test – to be supervised by the union *and* the state so that the union could not rig it. Rutgers learned of a secret test scheduled by the ironworkers. They moved to have it opened up and, together with NCE, insisted that NCC candidates take that test.

"But it will be a farce if the union has sole responsibility for that test," Home told Rutgers. "There is no way our candidates can pass. We will only agree if the contractors know about our candidates and take equal responsibility, and if you agree that our apprentices will be hired over any present apprentice list."

Rutgers finally agreed. Home, Eddie, and Derek Winans took the nine young Black men down to the ironworkers' hall to apply. As they drove up in Ed's Volkswagen bus, they could see that the yard was full of Cadillacs and Chryslers. They walked into a hall decorated with Republican election posters. The ironworkers stared in disbelief. It was as if Home and Eddie and their companions had come from outer space.

But the ironworkers found a loophole. They cancelled the test on the grounds that "there wasn't a quorum at the meeting that called it."

Rutgers then moved to get an opinion from the Attorney General as to whether it had legal standing to bring a charge of discrimination against the contractor. If so, it proposed to get a finding of "probable discrimination" from the Division of Civil Rights. Then Rutgers could hold that the contract was being violated unless the contractor immediately agreed to place nonwhite workers on the job, regardless of the wishes of the union.

"Eddie," said Home, "I think we have to move this out into the open. We've laid the groundwork. Now I think we have to reach for the state and put pressure on it to make sure Rutgers goes through with this agreement."

"How do you propose we do that? NCC doesn't have any political power. We going to take it to the streets?" Ed asked.

"Well, we may have to do that, too. But even though we don't have any power, power does exist in the community. Take all these Black elected officials. I think we ought to collect them and use their power to put pressure on the Man."

For the first time, *all* of the elected Black officials in Essex County, from freeholders to ward chairmen, were brought together — across party lines and political outlook — including some who never before in their lives had taken a stand. They came together to challenge Jim Crow in the building industry.

Borrowing power, though often tried, does not often succeed. One is always at the mercy of the lender. But this was an outstanding success. Agreement was reached to begin demonstrations on January 20 if Governor Richard J. Hughes refused to meet with NCC.

In the meantime, state officials moved to close down the protest. It was an election year, and the Governor was running for re-election. He had to keep things quiet while at the same time responding to the legitimate requests of the Black elected officials of his party. An assistant to Dean Heckel told NCC that Attorney General Arthur J. Sills had called and asked them to lay off the jobs fight in return for a promise to take the matter to a hearing before the Civil Rights Division.

"No dice," said Home. "A hearing will be no solution in a temporary job situation. The unions and the contractors will drag it out so long that the job will be over before anything is concluded. Immediate action is the only remedy. Rutgers must keep its commitment."

Realizing they weren't going to get anywhere with Home, the officials tried to get to Eddie alone. Eddie found Home at Dave Manning's bar and told him, "Home, the Attorney General wants me to call him. What do you think I should say to him?"

"Here it comes," thought Home. "Sills is trying to cruise my man out from under me. Before I tell him anything I better give him a little juice."

They sat talking and drinking, while Home told Eddie stories about the union. Ed kept making suggestions for dealing with the Attorney General, but each time, Home in effect rejected his idea by telling him about some other struggle and the tactics used.

"You know, Eddie," he said, "Hague always said there are three ways to deal with an enemy – win him over, seek to neutralize him, or if that doesn't work, move to kill. Sills is moving in on you."

Eddie kept pressing, "What should I do, man?"

Home finally shrugged his shoulders, took another drink, and said, "Tell him to go to hell."

Eddie wanted to show he was fully committed to the struggle, and so when the Attorney General called, he actually told him, "Go to hell."

On January 20, despite ten-degree weather, a picket line went up at the job sites. Black elected officials joined members of NCC on the line. The next day a call came from Governor Hughes, and the Black officials and NCC's negotiators gathered to go to Trenton.

In the warm-up meeting, Home said, "Look, this issue of Eddie telling the Attorney General to go to hell is bound to come up," and he told them the whole story. "But if we get caught up in that bit of business," he added, "we won't get anything accomplished, so we better have somebody ready to gait the dice."

Present at the meeting with the Governor were Ben Jones and Preston Grimsley of Orange, Councilman Irvine Turner, and Central Ward leaders "Honey" Ward (Democrat) and William Stubbs (Republican) from Newark, Freeholders Earl Harris and Charles Matthews, County Register Madeline Williams, Surrogate James Abrams, Home and Eddie from NCC, Dean Heckel of Rutgers, and the Attorney General.

The Governor opened, "So that we can start this meeting in good faith, I think Mr. Andrade should leave. I won't tolerate the way he talked to my Attorney General, nor will I tolerate him in this meeting."

"Honey" Ward jumped up. "Governor Hughes, we didn't come here to get involved in what went before. Let's not get hooked up in that. If you do, there's something to be said on both sides. I would have said the same thing myself, so let's get on with the meeting."

Others backed him. Eddie stayed. Hughes was asked: "Are you prepared to see that the state's commitment – that is, Rutgers' commitment – is kept? Will you back Heckel in taking the contractor before the Civil Rights Division on charges of discrimination?"

The Governor looked at Heckel. "Was there such an undertaking?"

"I wrote the Attorney General and asked if it was possible and he said yes, so we made a commitment to follow through on that policy."

The Governor looked at Sills. "Did you say that?"

Sills answered, "Yes."

"You are now released to keep any commitment you made," the Governor told Heckel.

Governor Hughes also agreed to call a meeting with the ironworkers. It was held, but the union refused to budge.

Rutgers filed with the Civil Rights Division, and NCC continued to push on the question of apprentices. The ironworkers held a test in the spring, but none of the young Blacks who took it passed, which did not surprise NCC.

NCC protested to Danzig, who equivocated and failed to act. He proposed public hearings. NCC immediately called the troops together for another meeting with the Governor, but this time, it was harder to get the elected officials together; it seemed to them as if a prestigious victory had been won, and public hearings would be a good compromise.

So NCC in October 1965 went to the meeting with the Governor with fewer people. No sooner had they walked in than the Attorney General took the offensive. He whipped out a paper and said he had the solution: public hearings, along with a no-demonstration clause. NAACP representatives reached to sign it. NCC and CORE refused.

NCC met the next day. Everyone present pledged to continue the fight and denounced the state's delaying tactics. "We told the state over and over that public hearings were not an effective remedy in a temporary job situation and that the *second* Rutgers building would be completed long before the hearings were over," Eddie reported. "Therefore, we would not voluntarily consent to an unworkable remedy when other remedies were available – including the state stopping the job."

But their hands were effectively tied by the NAACP's desertion of the struggle.

That night, the *Newark Evening News* ran a story on the

agreement to hearings and the non-discrimination clause. NCC retaliated with a white paper reviewing the history of the jobs fight, explaining their present position, and calling for a job and skills training center in the ghetto to prepare youth for jobs in the building trades.

The white paper concluded that, despite the setbacks, gains had resulted. NCC's efforts had produced one of the most representative job situations in Newark. Though the ironworkers did not yield, many of the trades had been forced to desegregate. NCC had pooled the strength of the Black elected officials for the good of the entire community. And they had forced the state to make important concessions in the enforcement of anti-discrimination laws.

It was a good fight, and a step ahead.

25   Redeem the Cities

HOME'S NEXT VENTURE into Newark began with the Tri-City Citizens Union for Progress. Initiated in 1967 by Black activists and churchmen from Newark, Jersey City, and Paterson, it was dedicated to "the common cause of Black empowerment." The idea had potential, but it needed a spark.

Newark was in a housing crisis. New highways, government buildings, and universities had eliminated much of the housing in the ghetto Central Ward, leaving mainly dilapidated and unsanitary dwellings.

Housing seemed a good issue for Tri-City, but where to begin? Experience with Freeway Development Corporation in Orange had shown that large plots of land and huge sums of money were needed for new housing.

Home asked Walter Barry, an old friend from UE who had moved to Orange, to investigate. A few days later, Walter came back with an idea.

"Why don't we go into rehabilitation work instead of new housing? New housing will take months of

Walter Barry.

negotiation before we can even start, and money is hard to get. But in rehab there's a wide-open field, and money is available through the Community Affairs Department and this New Jersey Housing Finance Agency which was just set up."

"Would we be able to do it on a large enough scale to have real impact?" Home asked.

"We can do it in a big way, and quickly. I think this is what we're looking for."

Dr. Harry Kingslow.

The plan was considered by Tri-City at its meeting early in 1967. State officials seemed only mildly interested. But July saw the Newark civil disorders. Almost immediately, state officials began to look again at the rehab proposal.

Tri-City Economic Union No. 1 was set up to handle the rehab work so that the whole organization would not be tied up in its economic aspects. The first problem was money. They had to show initiative by raising some capital before they could go to the state for a mortgage.

Priorities Investment Corporation was formed to garner the seed money, first from Home's supporters and friends in Orange – Dr. Harry Kingslow, Walter and his son Joseph Barry, Colson Woody – and later Vera B. McMillan and Carl Jones from Newark. Then they reached for Oliver Lofton, head of Newark Legal Services. Lofton became president of Priorities and Walter its director of projects.

The state, while expressing doubt about ultimate success, viewed the project favorably. It would look good, especially after the riot, to promote Black economic enterprise in the ghetto. Tentative agreement was given, but a condition was imposed that one entire square block be rehabilitated. This at first seemed impossible. Asked later what gave them the courage to do it, Walter Barry quipped, "Ignorance. Sheer ignorance."

As it turned out, however, there had been an exodus of whites from the South and West Wards. The turnover was so great that by 1970 those previously white wards were able to elect Black councilmen. Tri-City and Priorities looked for a possible block to rehabilitate in the West Ward and found one bounded by 18th and 19th Streets and by 19th and 20th Avenues. The area was not yet a slum, the houses were basically sound, and the residents were interested in selling. Walter Barry, who was white, secured the options on an individual basis so as not to arouse suspicion and drive sale prices up.

The state then set another provision before it would agree to a mortgage: Tri-City had to bring in the first house at 94 Nineteenth Avenue at the price proposed. Tri-City succeeded. The work began.

The first project, Amity Village I, consisted of ninety-eight units, mainly apartments in three-family houses. It was to be cooperatively owned and upon completion of rehab would be managed by Tri-City.

Hiring as many Blacks as possible was an aspect of the overall goal of the project – economic advancement of the Black community. A search was made for a Black general contractor,

Help Tri-City
Redeem the Cities!

AMITY VILLAGE

TRI-CITY CITIZENS UNION FOR PROGRESS

518 Springfield Avenue   Newark, N. J. 07103

Telephone: 242-1700

but few were available, and even fewer who could get bonded for a job of this size. Unable to find what they sought, Priorities became the general contractor in order to get state approval, and hired a Black supervisor. To become bonded, Priorities people had to sign personally and put their own savings and homes on their line.

When the project began, Black workers were hired at every job level, but it was difficult to find trained workers. The Newark Coordinating Council developed on-the-job training methods to help workers become proficient.

Tri-City played a role in helping to decide what the rehabilitated houses would be like. It held a conference of women to determine what they would prefer in an apartment in which they were going to live. Out of the conference came basic plans for remodeling – realignment of space to provide larger living rooms, color-coordinated kitchens and bathrooms, tiling, carpeting, wood paneling, dishwashers, air conditioning. The women said that since most of the apartments were railroad flats with one open bedroom, that room should be closed off for privacy.

Priorities' first approach was to make the houses livable but not to re-do everything. Work was limited to aluminum and asbestos siding, patch-plastering, new plumbing and new wiring, in addition to the improvements the women suggested. This policy proved unwieldy and was eventually abandoned. Priorities began to gut the houses – strip them down to the studs – and rebuild them altogether.

Since rehab costs almost as much as new housing, was it worthwhile? Priorities and Tri-City felt that it was important as part of a comprehensive program to save housing in the ghetto. Rehab could begin at the edges of the zones of the deteriorating housing, where structures were still sound. People could live comfortably in such houses for twenty-five or thirty years. In the meantime, older houses, closer to the center of the city, could be torn down and rebuilt.

One of the problems Tri-City faced throughout the project was keeping costs down to ensure that the economic load placed on tenant-cooperators would not be too heavy. The anticipated mortgage payment was set

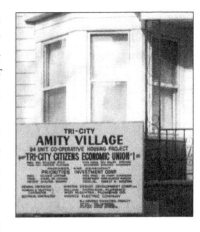

One of the rehabilitated homes.

at $135 per apartment. But the figure kept going up, partly because it had been set too low at the outset.

Frequently the non-profit sponsor in such a project was merely a rubber stamp, paid for rights to its name. The capitalists could thus run the costs up until they were out of reach of the poor who desperately needed decent housing. Tri-City, however, refused to be a rubber stamp and insisted that the interests of the people come first.

Without Tri-City to act as a brake, costs would have skyrocketed. The original $1.2 million mortgage rose to $1.4 million. Tri-City put its foot down.

"We ain't going this route no further," Home said. "Rather than spend any more of the people's money, we will shut the project down. Any more money you need will have to come from someplace else."

Finally, the state agreed to find the needed moneys. A grant of $100,000 and a loan of $50,000 which was later forgiven came to Tri-City from the Community Affairs Department.

The cost eventually ended up at $164 per apartment, but Tri-City was able to get rent and interest subsidies so that workers could afford the housing.

While Amity I was in process, plans had begun for Amity II, a much larger project. But by this time, the Republicans had come into power in the state, and there was a generally hostile attitude to community organizations and projects. The new administration did not like Tri-City's attempts to hold down the size of the mortgage and looked for excuses to close them down.

Priorities was not doing so well either. They were $200,000 in debt. At that point, North American Investment Corporation, a firm set up to take advantage of various tax write-offs for construction, offered to buy Priorities as well as Tri-City's interest in Amity II.

Walter Barry and Oliver Lofton presented the proposal to Home, who thought it sounded good. It seemed to him the right time to bail out. He agreed to support it provided the offer was put on paper and contained certain safeguards.

Home briefed the Tri-City leaders on what to fight for. Soon after, he entered the hospital for emergency surgery. He lay on the edge of death for weeks. From his hospital bed, he learned that practically everything he had warned Tri-City against was happening: North American was trying to make the deal in the name of Priorities, now a wholly-owned subsidiary which might fold at any minute. And there were rumors of reneging on the agreement to give Tri-City funds for an educational center.

Home called the Tri-City and Priorities representatives to his sickbed and said, "The deal's off."

In a series of stormy sessions in the weeks that followed, they worked out a new agreement. North American agreed to give

Tri-City a quarter of a million dollars, to be paid annually at the rate of $50,000 into a trust fund. They adopted the proposed guidelines on rent and a 40 percent minority work force. They also agreed to purchase and renovate a Ukrainian church in the Amity II area and rent it to Tri-City for its center, and to give Tri-City an option to co-op Amity II five years after its completion.

After three years of work, Priorities had successfully supervised the construction of the first housing rehab work in Newark, had erased its debt, and had been paid for its stock.

Tri-City had followed through on the precarious completion of Amity I and fulfilled its role as protector of the people. They could say they had made a commitment and kept it, ensuring the community would have some good, low-cost housing, some of it cooperatively owned. They had won some guarantees on how the white capitalist North American would operate in the ghetto in the future.

And for their trouble, they had reaped funds to expand their educational and health program and a center from which they could operate. A core staff was hired, and the work of the Tri-City People's Center began.

26 Crusade for Learning

ERNIE OFTEN REFERRED to Becky Andrade as a natural organizer, and he encouraged her to be active in education, one of the main needs of the people. She was a founder and later executive director of the Newark Pre-School Council, one of the largest community-run Head Start programs in the country.

Experiences with the educational system in Orange had shown that most children were not prepared to enter the world of work, and that many of the children of the poor were written off at an early age, forced to mark time, and either dropped or graduated as functional illiterates.

The educational crisis was even more serious in Newark, where the average sixth and seventh grade pupil was close to two years behind the national norm in reading and arithmetic. Newark schools, like those of other big cities, were totally unprepared for the waves of Southern migrants that brought a complete change in the student population in the 1960s.

The parents and staff who ran the Head Start program were rightfully concerned about follow-up for their children in the public school system. They helped organize a Crusade for Learning, launched at an educational conference in 1966 where Dr. Alexander gave the keynote address. The conference set out to answer several questions: What should Newark's policy be for preparation of students for the world of work? What kind of equipment was needed for an adequate education? How could parents and concerned citizens work to bring about needed change?

Millions of dollars were coming into Newark under Title I and were being squandered through bad planning, producing nowhere near the improvement a few thousand dollars had produced in Orange. The school administration was so resistant to community input that Crusade had to appeal to Black elected officials and the mayor to get a hearing with the Newark Board of Education. Crusade presented a plan to the board to ensure that these moneys were put to better use. They proposed concentration on the lower grades to provide quality early childhood education.

The superintendent refused to revise his plans, and the board was afraid to set policy to oversee the Title I program.

Parents then demonstrated and made enough noise that finally the New Jersey State Board of Education and the federal Office of Education came in to investigate their charges, instituting some of the changes Crusade for Learning had called for: kindergarten aides, a centralized planning staff to supervise Title I programs, follow-up Head Start, parent advisory committees, and medical follow-up.

The community did not have power to police the board of education, however, and those innovations were accordingly not carried out at a consistently high level.

A tutoring program to alleviate the immediate needs of many first- through seventh-graders was started in Madison Avenue School. That school was on split sessions, but even so, it was overcrowded, with as many as thirty-five or forty students in a class. Crusade for Learning brought in Professor Paul Mazurkiewicz of Newark State College, one of the nation's leading experts in i.t.a., to train volunteer tutors. Students were assigned to tutors on a five-to-one ratio and given remedial as well as tutorial help. Individualized attention was an important aspect of the program. On the whole, it was a good learning experience for the children who were involved.

In the summer of 1967, Crusade for Learning was the community sponsor of a Newark Board of Education tutoring program called Youth Helping Youth, based on the idea that older children with language and math deficiencies could improve their own skills while helping younger children with similar problems. Before starting the program, however, Crusade demanded that it have a say in the hiring of professional workers and that community people also be hired to supervise youth. This system guaranteed the youth – as well as the younger children – individual attention. On the worst day of the civil disorders of that summer, all youth tutors except one reported to work.

In 1968, after the Title I fight had gone as far as it could go and tutoring was underway, it was decided that the work of Crusade would be more effective if combined with a broader organization. Since many of those involved in Crusade were also active in Tri-City, Crusade became the educational arm of Tri-City.

The tutoring was moved to South Seventeenth Street School, in the Amity Village area. This required a long struggle with the school administration, which was jealous of anyone coming in to do the job it was supposed to be doing and wasn't. Crusade for Learning broke the roadblock by getting approval from the board of education. Every effort was made to give effective assistance to the children, and this was facilitated by a grant from the Episcopal Diocese, which helped Tri-City maintain an operational base.

But it became increasingly clear that if Tri-City was to have a real impact on education in Newark, it needed to develop its own educational center where it could carry out consistent programs, train staff, educate parents, and mobilize the community for quality education for all children. Tri-City set about doing this.

V. ON COALITION

...we could count and we knew what ten means in relation to ninety. Although we were proud of our prowess as Black men, we never figured no ten Black men could whip ninety white ones! So we decided we would need some help to raise that ten.

Coleman A. Young

27 Pure Coalition at Last

THE SCHOOL FIGHT in Orange had stirred up a great deal of anti-Black feeling. It was then that Nick Franco and others moved for charter change – back to the archaic and corrupt commission form.

CRG was caught on the defensive, in an unexpected role of having to protect the established form of government. They put together an alliance of some of the incumbents who were in favor of retaining the mayor-council form. Among the literature put out was a piece addressed to the East Ward which said: "Representative government at stake – fight to keep our representation." This was an important issue to the Blacks, who well knew they might not win if forced to run citywide. The whites in the coalition figured they would win either way, so they did not campaign aggressively.

In November 1969, the change of government election was held, and the bigots won. The clock was turned back six years. The victors immediately met with the city clerk to fix a date for the commission election, hoping to hold it the following March. This would crowd the incumbents and make it easier to displace them.

It was a sad moment for the Black community and a heavy defeat for CRG. Janeice Day, a young woman active with Becky Andrade in preschool education, telephoned Home, asking "What are we going to do now?"

"Janeice," Home replied, "we still got the people in the streets, and as long as we have the people, we'll be all right."

Cheered by Home's optimism, CRG and the incumbents threw their weight behind having the election in May – not March – to allow breathing time. CRG began to plan how to win at large.

A new situation prevailed from what existed in 1958 when Dr. Alexander ran. There was a larger Black population, including pockets in each ward and a sizeable number on the "hill." The Black community no longer danced to the tune of the keepers of the *status quo* – they had power and knew how to use it to form coalitions for the good of the city. They had played a decisive role in the first charter change, the high school fight, educational improvement, recreation, and housing. They had introduced new ways into Orange political life.

For the Black community itself, there had been many changes. Whereas before there had been no Blacks in many jobs, they now held jobs in every category. Where there had been a totally white board of education, now a Black person had been board president. Where Black teachers had been confined to Oakwood, now they were teaching in every school, and there were Black principals. And where there had been no representation in government, now the outstanding legislator and programmer on the council was Black.

Matters had also changed in the white community. The departure of older whites and the arrival of younger, less affluent residents had brought many who believed Blacks had a right to representation and were prepared to live with it. The white community had also witnessed various kinds of coalition over the past twelve years.

In order for Ben to win this citywide round, he would have to have a better coalition than ever. The incumbents were asked to run with him. Without exception, they declined.

Then Home asked Tom Kelly if he would run. After thinking it over for a few days, he stopped by Home's house. "Ernie," he said, puffing on his pipe, "I've decided to run. I don't think I could live with myself if I didn't. I would like you to help me put my campaign together."

Home agreed, and laid out the steps used by CRG in running a campaign.

Tom began by calling together his friends and acquaintances. Home went to the first meetings and explained to the whites the need for coalition. Among those who attended were Susan and Kevin Donnelly. They had met Ernie in 1968 during the Eugene McCarthy presidential campaign. Tom asked Kevin to be his campaign manager. Kevin, reluctant at first, finally agreed and then plunged into the Orange political scene. On St. Patrick's Day, Kelly, the Donnellys, and others were invited to the Kingslows' for what Kevin later called "the most Irish St. Patrick's Day of my life." They had spent the entire time discussing politics.

The Donnellys were impressed, not only because they met Blacks for the first time on an equal footing, but also because they found a group of people who were principled, yet at the same time were not afraid of power, and knew how to fight for it and how to use it. Kevin, a former seminarian, said, "They seemed to be truth in action. I felt at home because this was like the Irish tradition I knew."

With Tom in the race, the whole campaign took on a different aspect. This was no loose alliance, no defensive support of a white person: This was whole-hearted coalition, based on common interest in educating children and dealing with other problems of the city. Tom was on Ben's literature, and Ben was on Tom's.

The strategy that evolved was based on taking two big wards – the East, which was Ben's base, and the South, where

Kelly lived, which was one of the biggest areas of Black voters outside the East Ward. Between Tom's machinery and that of the Amalgamated Organizations, Ben and Tom figured to do well in the South Ward. It remained to pick up whatever Black support existed in the other two wards.

Ernie at his 59th Birthday Party, with (from left) John Alexander, Jimmy Murphy, and Larry Gordon.

There were two Black candidates besides Ben in the field, Morris "Shorty" Thomas and Bill Cook. "We have to balance our slate," said Home, "and we have to deal with these cats, even though we don't expect them to win. I think we'll be criticized if we don't endorse one of them. I recommend 'Shorty.' I also suggest we support Joel Shain, who is part of the Jewish community, an important part of the city.'"

Ben endorsed Shain, who did not reject the support but made it clear to the voters that he had not asked for it. Nevertheless, it was decided to stick with him. Rabbi Joachim Prinz, nationally known leader, who has spoken at the 1963 March on Washington, and a resident of Orange, and his wife Hilde sent out a letter to all the Jewish voters, endorsing Shain, Jones, and Kelly.

The campaign began with a big dinner honoring Ben. Percy Sutton, whom Ben and Home knew from the National Convention of Negro Elected Officials, spoke on coalition. "Orange," he said, "needs Ben Jones and Tom Kelly, and they stand ready to do a job for the people." He continued:

> When Black people enter political life, they must learn to be flexible, they must learn how to serve not only their community but the entire community... For when we join together with the Irish, the Italians, and the Puerto Ricans and all the others who make up this society, then we can begin to change it. Alone, we will never succeed.

> Orange needs the kind of coalition that Ben Jones and Tom Kelly bring. They have firm roots in their separate communities and come together on the basis of equality. Their strength and courage are the basis for coalition.

The campaigners saw Orange as a potential model city – economically and racially mixed, with typically urban problems – but on a scale that was open to solution. Perhaps Orange could be a testing ground for solving those problems through the leadership of a strong coalition.

Early in the campaign, it was discussed whether Jones and Kelly should travel separately or together. Separately, they could cover twice as much territory and talk to twice as many people. But it was decided that it was more important for people to see the coalition in action. They campaigned together.

Since Kelly had not held elective office, he ran – as Ben had seven years before – on the program for which he proposed to fight. But Tom's position was strengthened by Ben's seven years

For Vision, Courage and Integrity
ELECT

TOM KELLY
FOR CITY COMMISSIONER

Tuesday, May 12th, 1970

Elect... TOM KELLY **13A**
BEN JONES **12A**

of service and Tom's association with Ben's record through his work in the board of education, Legal Services, Orange Opportunity Corporation, Friendship House, and elsewhere.

At one coffee klatch given by Kevin Donnelly's landlord, a white worker, Tom took it for granted he had the host's vote, but he wasn't so sure where the man would stand on voting for Ben. After the meeting, the landlord came up to them and said, "Ben, I'm going to vote for you – I know you and I know you're good. But why should I vote for Kelly? I don't know him from Adam."

A high point in the campaign occurred during the protest against the invasion of Cambodia ordered by President Nixon. PACT, a youth peace group, called a demonstration for Orange Park and asked Ben to speak.

"That's good, Ben," said Home. "The young people deserve support. But more than that, they deserve a peaceful world. This country isn't going to straighten itself out until the war is over. They need your help and you need theirs. I think you should go make that speech."

When Ben got to the rally, he found about 200 young people. The police were out in force. Ben stuffed his prepared speech in his pocket and spoke from his heart. Some of the young people became interested in his campaign and later turned out to help. PACT endorsed Ben's candidacy.

It was a tough campaign, and there were many problems. Home was very ill and couldn't get around to check on organization. Literature was late; one piece couldn't be used because of a printing error. Money was scarce. Where other candidates were running campaigns on as much as $25,000, Ben and Tom had only a few thousand between them. But they stretched their funds, corrected their mistakes, and kept the campaign moving.

Ben Jones at a peace rally in Orange Park. "Bums" was Spiro Agnew's word for peace advocates. Photo by Herb Way.

It became clear that if any Black person could break through citywide, it was Ben. His record was outstanding and far surpassed that of any other candidate. And he had a strong, open coalition working for him in all wards.

Election day came. Home went to the doctor that morning with severe pain and was told to go into the hospital immediately. "Don't even go home for your things."

Home protested, "But I didn't vote yet."

The doctor shook his head. "If you vote, it may cost you your life."

The election results showed Ben tied with Quincy Lucarello for the fifth and last spot on the commission. When the news was brought to him in the intensive care unit, Home was even sicker to hear that his candidate hadn't won because of the vote *he* hadn't cast.

When the absentee ballots were counted, Lucarello came in ten votes ahead. It looked certain that Ben had lost. Kelly, Ben's partner in coalition, had gone down to defeat. People gathered at Doc's to discuss what could be done. One thing was sure – there had to be a recount. There was a feeling that the election had somehow been stolen.

Rudy Thomas.

Many were convinced that the recount would reveal the stolen votes in one of the white wards, but Rudy Thomas said, "I think we have to look in our own ward. That First District doesn't measure up to what it's been in any past election."

On recount day, Ben was checking the machines ward by ward – South, West, East… The woman reading the figures on the First District machine called out, "12A, Ben Jones, 177." The prior figure had been 77.

Ben gasped. Rudy jumped up and down, yelling, "Hold it, hold it, hold it!" He pounded on the table, "Don't you see?" he cried. "That's it, that's the election! Ben won!"

Not only had Ben won, but he moved into fourth place. The lost votes were right where Rudy had predicted they would be.

The final results showed that the people of the city wanted to move forward, not backward.

Ben had been victorious. Although Kelly had lost, credit for Ben's victory went to Tom and his committee for carrying the message of coalition to the white voters.

Shain, the first Jew elected in Orange, had won – and the support of the Jones-Kelly coalition had been decisive in the outcome.

Harry Callaghan and Carmine Capone, who had been in favor of retaining mayor-council form, were victorious.

Only one candidate who favored reverting to the commission, John Trezza, got into office.

The result was a fairly representative government – far better than any previous commission.

When the commission met to organize, Ben fought for Kelly to become city attorney and also threw his weight behind Shain for mayor. He was successful on both counts. Ben became Commissioner of Parks and Public Property, in charge of whole areas of programming that would vitally affect the Black community.

The oldest racist political tradition – that a Black person could not be elected to office in a citywide election where Blacks were a minority – had been shattered in Orange.

28 Coalition Old and New

On December 12 and 13, 1970, a reunion of the National Negro Labor Council was held in Cathedral House in Newark. Home was there, and Coleman Young and Vicki Garvin. Jack Burch and Ernie DeMaio of UE came in from Chicago. Morris Doswell came from New York. Alice and Harold Smith, Walter Barry, Bill Santora, Earl Williams, and Tom Edgerton came from New Jersey. Invited guests Reverend Ulysses B. Blakeley, Dr. John Alexander, Ben Jones, Eddie and Becky Andrade, Morton Stavis, and college students came.

Harold Smith, labor leader, who became a councilman in East Orange.

Coleman Young made the keynote speech, and Mindy Thompson gave a summary history of the NNLC.[13] The reunioners toured Amity Village, the Tri-City rehab project, and there was a cultural hour on Saturday night which presented excerpts from Lorraine Hansberry's *To Be Young, Gifted and Black.*

190

They played Paul Robeson singing "Joe Hill" and heard again the words,

> Where working men defend their rights,
> It's there you'll find Joe Hill...

Home's old and new friends were united in common dedication to liberation. It was a reaffirmation of the validity of the policies developed by NNLC from 1951–56. The leaders had retreated to the ghetto and come back strong, as they had promised. They discussed coalition and the working class, the tactics which had made it possible for them to survive.

Coalition, in particular, was on everybody's mind. Harold Smith started it off, saying, "We involved ourselves in coalition because we feel that this is the only true way, this is the only way we're going to be sure of going anyplace."

Ernie DeMaio added, "In the shop, where conditions get so bad, you have to fight the boss and you can only fight him with the guy that's alongside of you. And you don't ask the guy to help you win that fight because he goes to the same church you do or because he's the same color you are, or his grandfather came from the same country your grandfather came from. At that point it's an economic fight, and when it's an economic fight, you either fight together or you all lose together."

"We saw no contradiction," Jack Burch said, "in this question of having a Black organization and having unity with white workers. We saw no contradiction at all. On the one hand, we recognized the need of Black people in Black organizations – not separate unions, but organized into groupings to plan and discuss their interests, and to defend their interests. We also recognized that the same kind of repression in the plant against Negro workers applied to white workers, and therefore you had a kind of natural alliance if you could develop it."

Coleman Young took up the issue in greater depth in his keynote: "We saw among the white population our most natural and long-term reliable allies to be the trade union movement. We fought within that union and we fought the leadership of that union for our dignity, for our manhood, for our equality. At the same time, we fought to join with that union to move it into the struggle for Black liberation. And twenty years later, I would say that this is still a valid approach."

The meeting took on another dimension with the discussion of women's rights. Since NNLC had had an advanced policy on this question, it was a major area of consideration at the reunion. From opening comments on NNLC's work, discussion shifted to the state of the movement today. Differences were pointed out by the women students: One expressed the idea that much of the present movement has adopted an individualistic, social explanation of women's oppression, ignoring the economic basis. Another defended the present women's movement, "I think that there's a tendency to minimize the social and sexual oppression of women, and I don't think it is minimal. That's why women can be oppressed economically – because they're considered worthless in every other way."

"Yet," added a third, "the social – sexual – economic exploitation of Black women has not been the same as that of white women. The Black woman has had to get out and work."

"I think the issue here is the narrowness of the movement," said Dr. Alexander. "The women's movement is now fighting almost exclusively over the abortion issue, when they ought to be fighting over the total health problem, because abortion is only part of the health problem... It's a natural coalition of women's lib, Blacks, Chicanos, the poor, and others, in coalition with labor, to make demands on this wealthy country to provide the basic health care needs of everybody, irrespective of their ability to pay."

Home at last took the floor, saying, "I would like to call to your attention that we had a phenomenon in the UE on this point. When we brought the Black leaders together, we said, 'we can't win nothing in this union if we don't coalesce.' And so we were the conscious leaders of the coalition of women and Blacks. One thing was proven, that if white male leadership had neglected the woman question, Black leadership could organize the women if they wanted to.

"One of the things we did in Orange was to base ourselves primarily on women. Our position was, 'if we don't be having these women, we don't be having no movement.' The backbone of the twelve years of that struggle was the women.

"The women's movement in the United States has a vast potential. We understood that when we went to Louisville."

He urged that Blacks once again become conscious partners in coalition with the women's movement.

Perhaps the most important thought was expressed by Harold Smith: "I would like to see another organization such as the NNLC come into being. It will be a lot younger people than us, of course... But we struggled, and I think we made our impact upon America. I know we made our impact; I was on that airlines picket line out in Cleveland in 1952.

"We need this type of organization. I believe in the philosophy and principles of the NNLC, and I think they are just as valid today as they were fifteen years ago when we disbanded or twenty years ago when we started."

What We Learned

POWER FOR THE POWERLESS has been our goal during our twelve years in Orange. Our experience has proven that the powerless can win power and enter the central arena to fight for their own urgent democratic needs, as well as for the needs of all people. I want to summarize here the lessons of these years of struggle so that they will be helpful to the powerless all over the country.

When we began in Orange twelve years ago, we based ourselves firmly on the ghetto – the source of all our strength. We first built a coalition on the liberation front, by bringing together the Black middle-professional and working classes to work for their common democratic needs. Neither class had representation; neither had a say in the cutting of the pie. Historically, the small number of Blacks in most cities had been forced to go hat-in-hand and speak through those with training, mainly the middle class.

But now the great increase in Black population in the cities and the growing consciousness of the rights of the Black people laid the basis for something more. The classes of Blacks could come together and demand control of areas with Black majorities. White politicians who previously had only contempt for the Blacks now had to contend with a real force.

The power we acquired in Orange through control of the Democratic Party in the ward and through Citizens for

Representative Government was mainly in the hands of the working class. It was just and reasonable that the working class, as the majority, should be in control of the machinery. The workers knew what discipline, exploitation, and struggle meant; the middle class did not. At the same time, we tried to use the skills and training of middle class Blacks to maximize their contribution. Our leaders were sensitive to this problem and struggled to prevent the middle-professional class from taking control of the movement.

Having recognized the problem of leadership, it was not sufficient for the growing machinery of Black control to sit idling in the ghetto. To solve the problems of the ghetto, it was necessary to go into the central arena, to go where decisions are made. Just as General Electric and General Motors are not controlled in the ghetto, neither are school systems. If we wished to improve the school system, to guarantee that our children would be prepared for the world of work, we had to fight for representation on the Board of Education.

In moving out of the ghetto, we knew that we had to multiply our strength, to find allies. In every struggle, we emphasized coalition. We brought to these coalitions our organization in the ward, and our influence in the Democratic Party and the labor movement.

The power base for a coalition must never be forgotten. One of the danger spots in coalition politics is to forget that it is the organization of *your own* base, which is the sole force with which one moves into a coalition.

Coalition, furthermore, is based on common interest. If a coalition succeeds, it is because each of the groups within it succeeds as well. In the fight for education, we fought for all children. We could not have won had we fought only for the education of Black children. If we had lost, the white children would have lost, too. White children are also a part of the 80 percent destined to go to work without further training after high school. We made this clear when we presented the issues: We tried to base ourselves on the widest base, rather than the narrowest. We raised our battle cry for a good high school because we believed that every person should have a right to dignity and a place in this society.

Yet there were those who called for separatism, wishing to appeal only to the Black minority, through Vote-Black campaigns.

History has shown this to be an untenable position. With the abolition of slavery, which was in fact a main cause of the degradation of *white* labor, the movement for union organization and agitation for the eight-hour day swept the country. A national labor organization, the National Labor Union, was formed. One of its great defects was that it did not admit Black workers or fight for their right to be in unions. In so doing, white workers harmed their own cause. The progress of the labor movement was held back until white workers and labor leaders recognized this point.

Blacks, in reaction to exclusion from white unions, formed their own organization, the National Colored Labor Union. Many times, Black workers had to go on strike separately from white workers. But they could not confront the boss apart from white workers because he would use that division to destroy them both. Their movement ended in failure.

It happened over and over again that Black people were excluded from organizations in every area of life. Until they could in some way have an impact on those organizations, they were left out in the cold. This was true of the Democratic Party as I saw it in Hudson County and later in Orange; it was true of government, labor unions, and fraternal organizations.

Black people did not originally *choose* separatism; it was thrust upon them. But history proved that they could not hope to improve their situation by remaining separate. As we found in Orange, decisions are not made in the ghetto and cannot be changed there. Separatist politics only aid and abet the separation forced on Black people in the past.

In Orange, where the Black population was small, it was a hopeless tactic. Dr. Alexander could not be elected in 1958 even with a coalition with sections of the labor movement – because he did not have broad enough support in the white community.

But even if he had been elected, what could his one vote have done? Against it, there would have been the votes of the four white commissioners.

When Ben was elected councilman, the question remained: What could his one vote do? We needed to have an impact on the mayoralty and at-large elections and to build a coalition with councilmen from other wards. When Ben sat on the seven-member council, he had to be able to count on four votes, not just his own.

So we learned that coalition on the liberation front was not enough; we needed coalition in the central arena, too. We found various bases for common struggle. In the charter change fight, we formed a coalition with Republicans, Democrats, and labor; in the council, we had coalition based on the Democratic Party.

After the second charter change election in 1969, the need for coalition became even more clear. Ben had to win at-large. The Black voters alone could not determine the outcome of the election. The support of Tom Kelly and his organization was crucial to that victory.

What was the difference in our position between 1958 and

1970? There were two important differences. One was the fact that in 1958, we were a powerless, unrepresented section of the city. By 1970, we had become a powerful organized force in city government, able to coalesce with those who were interested in our programs – education, housing, recreation. In addition, we could fight on the special problems of our community, including the right to buy land, putting Black doctors on the staff of Orange Memorial Hospital, etc.

The other important factor was the change in the white community with respect to Blacks. Whites like Kelly had learned that coalition was the effective policy and that, together, we could bring in the goods. And the white community itself was changing – younger, less affluent, prepared to accept coalition. This objective historical shift prepared the way for the subjective shift: It laid the groundwork for what we call *pure* coalition.

Pure coalition is wide-open coalition on the basis of complete equality of Black and white, with the working class as the main base. This is the ultimate in coalition and must be the kind of coalition built in this country.

In the struggle to build pure coalition, we learned many lessons. When we came to the fight, no one gave us any guarantees that it would last a day or a week or a year. Sometimes we saw problems that we had no immediate way of solving. This was the case with the Oakwood gerrymander; it was the case when we first saw the reading and failure rates.

Before we could move out, we had to prepare. Politics is not a game; it is an occupation for 365 days a year. And it is unending. We have worked in Orange for twelve years, and the struggle goes on as you read these words.

Our experiences – the lessons of this book – are desperately needed in today's world to help humankind learn to live together. The NNLC twenty years ago made its commitment to this cause. We spread from coast to coast the words of Dr. Mordecai Johnson, an outstanding fighter for peace in America, then president of Howard University. We took his message to the masses through the keynote speeches at two of our national conventions. Reading his words again today, we can more fully appreciate the prophesy he made then about the future of the United States:

> If we look at ourselves in the way that history shows it to us, we are probably the most ruthless dominators and exploiters and humiliators of human life that ever spanned the pages of history.
>
> For all of a hundred years now, we have had in our hands scientific and technical intelligence, the most creative weapon of economic and political constructiveness that ever came into the hands of men. We have shown what we could do with that weapon by building up the great economic and political structure of the United States, and Britain, France, Germany, and Japan.
>
> But for 200 years, while we have had it in our power to build up likewise the economic and political freedom of Africa, China, Malaya, Indo-China, and the peoples of the Near East, we not only have not done so, but we have used that very power to conquer them in war, to dominate them politically, to exploit their natural resources and their labor, and to segregate and humiliate them upon the land upon which their fathers have died, and in the presence of the graves which hold the bodies of their mothers.
>
> I tell you that the man we have met at the crossroads of

history, and who is making that question to us, is not in the first instance the people of Asia and Africa, or the people of Russia, but the Eternal God himself.

Says God, "Why did I bring you up from being the scum of the earth and outcasts of Europe, despised and rejected, to make you the most resourceful, intelligent and great organizing genius of the human race, with reserve capital unparalleled in the human race? Do you think I have brought you to such a place that by order of the use of this power you would seize and control and dominate and inhibit and choke vast numbers of men who like yourselves are hungering for the liberty and security you have, and have just as much right to it as you have, because they are my sons?"

I believe with Dr. Johnson that the United States is at the crossroads. And time has run out. It has run out on us morally in the eyes of humankind and in the eyes of God.

We have no more time for war, or exploitation, or poisoning the earth. We must learn to live together now.

The problem in the United States of people living together is a Black-white problem. The separatists – be they Black or white – only obstruct our way. They have no answers for the tasks confronting us.

These tasks are too crucial to be entrusted to the warmongers and the profiteers. The money-changers must once again be driven from the temple so that the people can prevail, for only the people can be entrusted with their own future.

This is what we attempted to do in Orange, as one step in the long march toward people learning to live together. I believe, as Albert E. Kahn, another fighter for peace, once said:

People like ourselves want a world in which the bitter and needless weeping of children will end. And we are not alone. Throughout the whole length and breadth of the earth, there are countless millions of human beings who are determined to have a different and a better world.

Our hands, the hands of the American people, are linked with their hands; their strength is ours.

We not only want that better world; we demand it, and we will build it – a world of peace, a world of joy, a world rid of the weeping of children, *a world in which the laughter of children will resound on every side and in every land...*

—Ernest Thompson
Orange, New Jersey
January, 1971

Postscript to the First Edition

IN THE FIVE YEARS since Ernie wrote those words, the citizens of Orange lost many of the gains they fought for.

In 1974, there was another commission election. Ben Jones and Tom Kelly ran in coalition, but both were defeated – Ben by the narrow margin of eighty-four votes. The Black community permitted itself to be split; there was a certain complacency on the part of Ben and his campaign; and the Democratic Party machinery failed to provide support to the coalition.

There was also evidence of irregularities. A grand jury investigated the election, looking into charges that out-of-town residents had been permitted to vote. Ben and Tom brought suit in the Superior Court of New Jersey to overturn the election, but the case was dismissed, the court refusing to let them use the grand jury minutes to buttress their contentions.

With Ben out of office, Blacks lost their voice in government. It took time for the message to sink in. It showed up first in municipal jobs. City Hall was integrated when Ben left office; within three or four months, it reverted to being almost all white.

It showed up in appointments, with the Black community having lost the right to have an input.

It showed up in neglect and deterioration of programs important to Black and working people, which Ben had developed.

Two stages of construction had been completed at Colgate

Park – a facility as much needed by whites in the North Ward as by Blacks – and federal funds had been allocated to finish the final stage. Nothing further was done after Ben left office. So, too, nothing further was done to build a new Friendship House.

The outreach program in venereal disease, tuberculosis and lead poison testing, sickle cell screening, and diabetes detection was eliminated. The annual Health Fair at the Alexander Homes, a low-income project in the East Ward, is now held in a bank, practically guaranteeing it will not reach those who need it. The administration allowed the public health nurses to discontinue home visits and made the Baby-Keep-Well Station a perfunctory operation.

The drug abuse program had been an example to the rest of the country. It dealt with drug abuse as a health rather than a criminal problem. It is no longer city-sponsored and has to scrounge for funds to provide minimal services.

Although Ben had been the moving force in securing senior citizen housing for the city, there has been a sharp drop-off in the number of Black senior citizens admitted to the housing.

On March 24, 1975, indictments were announced, for charges ranging from extortion to false swearing, against Public Safety Commissioner Quincy Lucarello, Police Chief Eugene Urcoli, eight other police officers, and a fire captain. Trial of one defendant ended in mistrial; trial of another resulted in hung juries on two occasions. The balance of the defendants have not been tried.

A grand jury presentment recommending that Orange abandon its commission government for a system with more effective checks and balances gave rise to a government-change movement. The League of Women voters gave leadership, with the help of the Orange Tenants Association and clergy.

There was a referendum on the November 1975 ballot, which

resulted in a two-to-one victory for mayor-council reform. Elections for a mayor and seven council members (four ward representatives and three at-large) are scheduled.

Both Ben Jones and Tom Kelly are running for office, Ben for East Ward Councilman and Tom for Councilman-at-large. It is hoped that they and other candidates with vision will be elected and will work in coalition to deal with the pressing needs of Orange's people.

Tri-City, on the other hand, has achieved stability. It brought together many old friends: Becky and Eddie Andrade and Doris Williams on staff, Dr. Alexander and Vera McMillon as trustees, Tom Kelly as attorney, Milton Zisman as accountant. Reverend Dr. Ulysses B. Blakeley and Maso Ryan, founding members, Dan Brown, a former Amity I resident, and Maggie Thompson serve on the board with people from the neighborhood.

The coalition is working.

Tri-City has remodeled its People's Center. It has a full-day child care center, which the state considers a model of excellence. Its kindergarten and after-school program welcomes children from the South Seventeenth Street School with a hot lunch and provides them with an educational program, recreation, and custodial care for the balance of the day. The remodeled building will permit Tri-City to have its own food service and a nutritional program embracing the community. In a separate building, a mini-clinic provides a wide range of health services to women and children in the neighborhood. Health block workers will shortly be working in the twelve-square-block concentration area.

Tri-City cannot participate in partisan politics, but it intends to guarantee that every potential voter in its target area is registered. Eddie Andrade is in charge of the economic development of

Tri-City and its concentration area. Within those boundaries, Tri-City owns and/or manages approximately 300 units of the housing renovated by Priorities Development Corporation. Approximately 100 are cooperatively owned; the balance will be encouraged to become cooperative. Residents are being trained in management, maintenance, repair, and construction. All jobs are open without bias as to sex; in fact, the resident manager of the housing is a woman.

Through Becky Andrade, Tri-City has been involved in coalition building by coordinating the efforts of numerous day care centers and agencies concerned with children, in a campaign for "Everything They Need to Grow," which fights for adequate funding, improved standards, and complete health care for children.

Plans almost without number to improve the area and the lives of its people are on the drawing board. Tri-City has shown that money can be found and that the community will respond. Expansion is limited only by the time required to find and train people who will dedicate themselves to its principles and help to build a showcase which will point the way to redeem the cities.

—Mindy Thompson
April, 1976

Postscript to the Second Edition

I WAS ACTIVE IN THE Peace Movement during the fight against the war in Vietnam. I constantly called my father to ask for advice. He always had wise thoughts, and managed to keep me out of trouble through those years. He, too, was responding to the times, and ran as a McCarthy delegate during the Eugene McCarthy campaign in 1968. He shared with me that he wanted to support the young people – liberal young whites – who had come to town and were beginning to organize.

It turns out that this bridge played a crucial role in saving the city. One of the young people who came to town was Patrick Morrissy, who later founded Housing and Neighborhood Services (HANDS), a community development corporation that played a crucial role in staving off the worst harms of contagious housing destruction. Pat found ways to take the most difficult problem properties, untangle their legal problems, restore their physical structure, and put them back to work, housing community leaders. While many other rustbelt cities burned to ground, Orange teetered, but did not go up in flames.

On the political front, as the African American population grew to be a majority of the city, they moved into all the positions of leadership. The challenges of running a postindustrial city were many, from the crumbling infrastructure, to the limited tax base. In 2007, when I started to re-engage with the area, the city again needed an organization that would organize the powerless – this time, immigrants recently arrived in the area who had limited English and no political power.

But what I also recognized was that Orange was a remarkable place. By then I'd visited cities all over the world and understood what were the components of the modern city. As I traveled around Orange, I realized that the city had one or more of each of those elements, and typically designed by a major architect. These included a library designed by the firm of McKim, Mead & White, a park and subdivision designed by the firm of Frederick Law Olmstead, a pastoral cemetery in the style of Mount Auburn in Boston (and created about the same time) and a Colonial-era graveyard, surrounding the First Presbyterian Church, founded in 1741.

Orange also had an array of markers of class and race oppression: the mansions of the wealthy in one part of town; the small working-class houses surrounding the factories, now shuttered and bleak; a highway shoved through the Black and Italian neighborhoods in the middle of town; and an empty community hospital, once the proud place of succor for the city's residents.

That year, 2007, was a grim time for the city, as the Great Recession took off, stopping many of the development projects then poised to start. The Mayor was indicted for corruption, and the foreclosure crisis began to undermine much of the city's housing stock. It was in recognition of all that had happened and was happening in Orange that we got the idea to start the University of Orange, truly meant to be a way to learn from the city-as-university. Patrick Morrissy, Molly Rose Kaufman, and I were among the enthusiastic group that gathered in 2008 to start a free people's university. This book is being reissued in 2018, as the University of Orange celebrates its tenth anniversary.

Ernest Thompson succeeded in his lifetime in building a bridge to the next generation of organizers. He had an even bigger vision: to touch the youth of the future through the pages of his book. His experience had demonstrated, time and time again, that coalition was the method for the powerless to regain power. In the poem, *The Bridgebuilder*, an old man returns to build a bridge across a chasm. Ernie, having crossed many rough streams in his day, turned back to write this book, leaving it as a bridge for his readers to travel to a better future.

—Mindy Thompson Fullilove
January, 2018

Afterword

I HAVE READ *Homeboy Came to Orange* many times over the years for many reasons. As a child, I wanted to see the names of my family in print and find the childhood photos of my mother, Mindy. After my grandmother passed, I wanted to find her in these pages. I retold all the Maggie stories to others, expanding them to represent her true heroism. When I first started working as a community organizer in Orange, I wanted to understand anything and everything about the streets I walked. Reading the book now, to write this epilogue, I am awed by Ernie's capacity to understand systems and operate the levers of influence while bringing the people along with him. I am awed by his ability to create space for others to lead, to serve, to live with dignity and power.

I finished journalism school at Columbia University in 2007. I had trained to be a print reporter just as newspapers were folding around the country. I had some time on my hands. My mom wanted to understand the legacy of my grandparents and their community. When she'd visited Orange after many years, she saw that the work of Ernie, Maggie, Ben, Becky and their colleagues and friends had created a strong foundation for the city. Though facing challenges, the city was in better shape than it should have been given the full-on assaults US cities had faced in the second half of the 20th Century: urban renewal, deindustrialization, highway construction, mass incarceration and disinvestment. What had happened in Orange, Mindy wondered, and why was it still standing? Mindy recruited me to spend some time with her getting the story. In our family, we put each other to work.

We attended a 50th anniversary party celebrating the fight to desegregate the schools. Maggie lived in Hoboken when I was growing up and my mom's life had only rarely brought us back to Orange. So it was entirely unexpected to be standing at a party in a church and suddenly know that this was where I was going to be working, to feel that I had walked into my place. The event was co-hosted by HANDS, a neighborhood planning and affordable housing organization whose founder, Pat Morrissy, had been brought to Orange in part because of the legendary work of Ernie.

At the party, Pat asked me what I would be doing next in my life and I thought, "What a strange question. I am going to be working for you."

Indeed, a few months later I was hired by HANDS as a community organizer. One day, after walking around interviewing people for an oral history installation, I said to Pat, "So many people in Orange are in the businesses their grandparents started, Rossi Paint, Woody Home for Services . . ."

"You," he said.

In 2008, Mindy, Pat, Karen Wells, Jody Leight, Yielbonzie Johnson and I started a center for popular education, the University of Orange. The guiding questions were simple and powerful. What if we think of the city itself as a university, if we acknowledge that everyone has something to teach and everyone has something to learn? What if we lift up the message that you can learn the whole history of US cities in Orange, New Jersey? This is how we described UofO on the invitation to our convocation on November 9: *The University of Orange is committed to making Orange, New Jersey, THE urban village of the 21st Century, a place of justice, beauty and full employment! Through the UofO, we will amass the knowledge we need to reach this wonderful goal. In the streets, buildings and people of Orange, we can read the history of the American city and we can invent an inclusive future.*

We take very seriously the lessons of those who came before us, Ernie and the others who appear on the pages of this book. Being programmatic and working in coalition are without a doubt the most important skills we need in these times. We stay oriented by focusing on what we're *for* and we are studying the lessons of coalition in *Homeboy* and elsewhere. We have developed an urbanism department that applies these lessons to urban situations everywhere. We have written neighborhood plans, worked with middle school students to write a textbook about the city, and have nurtured a new generation of city leaders. People visit us from around the world to share their stories and struggles.

We also realize that "building people's power" means that people – individuals – come to claim their own abilities and power. This is where our free classes come in. People have volunteered to teach classes such as English as a Second Language, podcast making, beer making, guitar, music theory and what makes a great public space. To graduate we ask that people vote (non-governmental elections are acceptable since many are excluded from the governmental process), volunteer, attend a city meeting, have fun with their neighbors and take two courses (independent studies are welcome).

We are entering our tenth year as a free people's school. I am fortunate to get to work with the most motivated, dedicated team imaginable. Here are a few of the practices that I learned from Ernie, Maggie, Ben, and others that I try to pass along:

Show Up

When we first started the University of Orange we were beyond fortunate that Maggie Thompson and Ben Jones were still with us in their physical bodies on this earth. They were in their late 80s/early 90s with all of the ailments and battle scars that come with lives so long lived. Yet they showed up. To every meeting. With good attitudes and ideas, willing to make speeches or take

Top and opposite: Maggie Thompson and Ben Jones enjoying lunch and a joke at the Harris Diner. Photos by Mindy Fullilove.

notes. How many meetings in Orange, New Jersey, have they attended in their lives? As my grandmother said, "You've got to get out of your living room and be in the streets where the people are. What are you going to do in your living room? Watch TV?"

Be like Ben

Ben Jones used to greet everyone with a huge smile and say, "How you be?"

Ben was kind. Ben believed in other people. He also said that there should never be an event with a ticket price a regular person can't afford. And he was committed to serving those who had the least. He was committed to the benefits of physical activity and when he served on the city council he raised funds to build new public pools in Orange. At one point Orange had the most outdoor pools per capita of any city in the United States. Ben opened the first of the six pools in the Walter G. Alexander housing project, to show the city's solidarity with the people there, the "least of these."

Enjoy the barbecue

As a young organizer sometimes I worried that I was having too much fun. I was always making sure that our meetings and events had great food. We celebrated everyone's birthday with cake and spent lunch hours finding the best beef patties in the city. I expressed my fears to my mother. Aren't organizers serious and angry? It's not that I don't take my work seriously but…? My mom told me that one time, in the middle of a difficult campaign, Ernie and the union organizers were relaxing and eating barbecue when the head of their union walked in. The guys were embarrassed but their leader said, "Isn't this what are we fighting for? Food and drink and laughter?"

Tell the story

At the University of Orange we record and share stories of Orange to disrupt the dominant narratives that write off the city and its people. I have seen the power of what happens when we tell our own stories. One way has been through sharing *Homeboy Came to Orange*. Donna Williams, a local councilwoman will call me sometimes and say something like, "Can you bring a copy of the book to the fire station? Derek's grandmother is in it and he's never seen it." And I see people hold their city and their struggles in their hands.

As I reread this book this past few days, I sometimes felt a sort of stunned sickness that we are still here. We are still talking about the police murdering black people in the streets, still debating nuances of the women's movement and fighting for space for intersectionality. We are faced by ugly reality that workers have fewer rights and fewer of our children are being adequately trained to participate in our economy. I wonder what Ernie would say that we are still having these same conversations, if it would break his heart. And then I think how glad he would be that we are still having these same conversations. We have not given up. We will not give up. We don't have to make ourselves or our demands smaller.

My grandfather wrote the postscript to his book in January, 1971, 47 years ago. It says on the last pages of his book:

> We have no more time for war, or exploitation, or poisoning the earth. We must learn to live together now... These tasks are too crucial to be entrusted to the warmongers and the profiteers. The money-changers must once again be driven from the temple so that the people can prevail, for only the people can be entrusted with their own future. This is what we attempted to do in Orange, as one step in the long march toward people learning to live together.

We are still attempting in Orange. Join us.

—Molly Rose Kaufman
January, 2018

Endnotes

1. Brown, Sterling A., "Strong Men," *Southern Road: Poems by Sterling A. Brown*, Harcourt, Brace, and Company, NY, 1932, pgs. 51-53.

2. W.E.B. Du Bois, "Behold the Land," Address to the Southern Youth Legislature, October 20, 1946, Columbia, South Carolina.

3. Paul Robeson, "Forge Negro-Labor Unity for Peace and Jobs," National Trade Union Conference for Negro Rights, June 10, 1950, Chicago, Illinois. Reprinted in: *Paul Robeson Speaks: Writing, Speeches, and Interviews, a Centennial Celebration*, Citadel Press, NY, 2002.

4. Frances Gulotta, Remarks, *UE Convention Proceedings*, 1955, p. 185.

5. Ernest Thompson, Remarks, *National Negro Labor Council Proceedings of the Founding Convention*, Cincinnati, Ohio, October 27-28, 1951, p. 9.

6. William Hood, Remarks, *National Negro Labor Council Proceedings of the Founding Convention*, Cincinnati, Ohio, October 27-28, 1951, pgs. 12-18.

7. Coleman Young, "These Things We Fight for Will Be Ours," Keynote Address, Third Annual Convention, National Negro Labor Council, December 4-6, Chicago, Illinois.

8. "Un-Americans Subpeona Hood, Young, Rice, Other Detroit Unionists," *Daily Worker*, February 19, 1951, p. 1.

9. House Un-American Activities Committee, *Hearings on Communism in Detroit, I*, p. 2892.

10. News Release, New Jersey Negro Labor Council, undated.

11. Ernest Thompson, Remarks, *UE Convention Proceedings*, 1955, pgs. 199-201.

12. Will Allen Doomgoole, "The Bridgebuilder," in *Father: An Anthology of Verse*, EP Dutton and Company, NY, 1931.

13. Mindy Thompson, *A History of the National Negro Labor Council, 1951-1956*, Bryn Mawr College, Honors Thesis, 1971.

Index

Page references followed by *p* indicate an illustration or photograph.

abortion issue, 192
Abrams, James, 164
ACLU, 146
Addonizio, Hugh J., 71, 72
Ad Hoc Committee for a New High School, 148–149
AFL (American Federation of Labor), 6
AFL Foundry Workers strike, 7–8
AFL Foundry Workers Union, 7
airline industry, 27, 29
Alexander, Emmy Lou, 52, 118
Alexander, John ("Doc")
   appointed to school board and development of desegregation plan, 116–120; asked to run for office and New Day campaign of, 52–69; at Ernie's 59th birthday party, 183*p;* forming coalitions and other efforts to improve education, 94, 121–123, 127–147, 148–149, 153, 154*p;* NNLC reunion (1970) attended by, 190; reaffirming potential of Black leadership, 75; speeches given by, 83–84, 86–87, 113*p*, 120, 176; as Tri-City trustee, 204
Alexander, John (son of "Doc"), 52
Alexander, Kevin, 52
Alexander, Robert, 52
Alexander, Walter G., 51
Amalgamated Organizations for Good Government, 142–144
American Negro Congress, 21
American Radiator plant (Bayonne), 6–7, 10
Americans for Democratic Action (ADA), 160

Amity Village I project, 169–173, 174
Amity Village II project, 173–174
Andrade, Edward (Eddie), 96, 158–160, 161, 163–164, 175, 190, 204
Andrade, Rebecca Doggett. *See* Doggett, Rebecca

Bankston, Wendell, 54
Barringer High School site, 159
Barry, Joseph, 168
Barry, Walter, 167*p*–168, 169, 173, 190
Bergman, Leibel, 111*p*
"Big Train." *See* Thompson, Ernie
Black leadership
   commitment and accomplishments of the, 39, 50–58, 70–82, 124–147; Doc's appointment to the school board supported by, 116–120; indictments (1975) made against several, 203; lessons learned from Orange experiences of, 194–201; postscript to the first edition on outcomes of, 202–205; postscript to the second edition on outcomes of, 206–208; *See also* CRG (Committee for Representative Government) [later Citizens for Representative Government]; National Negro Labor Council (NNLC); politics; Thompson, Ernie
Black women
   social, sexual, and economic exploitation of, 192; working to protect rights of, 27, 32–33, 63, 108*p; See also* white women
Black workers
   building bonds between professional and, 64–65; CRG's building trade training program for, 98–99; excluded from white unions and challenges facing, 14–16, 98, 196–197; labor movement lessons and successes of, 7–9, 12–13, 24–25;UE's Black caucus membership of, 15–17, 19–20; *See also* labor movement
Black–white coalitions
   to improve education for all children and new high school, 127–155; Jones–Kelly coalition (1970), 180–189, 197–198; lessons learned from experiences in Orange and, 194–201; NNLC founding convention (1951) support of, 22–26; NNLC reunion (1970 attendees

reviewing benefits of,190–193; rejecting separatist polities and replacing with, 197, 200; working toward needed, 15–20, 179; *See also* Coalitions; politics; power; white politicians

Blakeley, Reverend Ulysses B., 190, 204

Board of School Estimate, 148

Brady, Father Charles, 153

Braun, William, 85–86, 87, 117

"Bridgebuilder" (poem), 95–96, 208

Brown, Dan, 204

Brownell, Attorney General, 34, 36, 38

Brown, James, 148, 153, 155

Brown, Molly, 53*p*, 54

Brown, Rich, 55

building trades
NCC's promotion of job democracy in Newark, 158–166; planned Rutgers Law School and NCE projects, 159, 160–162; training programs to help Blacks enter the, 98–99

Burch, Jack, 190, 191

California Test of Mental Maturity, 121

Callaghan, Harry, 144, 148, 153, 155

Cambodian invasion, 186

Capone, Carmine, 144, 147, 148, 152–153, 154, 155

Carey, Dennis F., 72, 94

the cat and the fox story, 54–56

Central Elementary School (Orange), 83–87

Central Ward (Newark), 73, 158, 164, 167

Chamber of Commerce, 152

Charlie, Mr., 61, 64

Charter Change Association
formation of the, 77; purpose and change achieved by, 77–82

CIO (Congress of Industrial Organization)

CIO Hudson County Industrial Union Council, 11

CIO-PAC (Political Action Committee)
formed by, 11, 53; Doc's campaign coalition with, 66–67; vicious attacks (1950s) against, 15; Wayne County, 22; *See also* UE (United Electrical, Radio and Machine Workers of America)

CIO-PAC (Political Action Committee), 11

Citizens and Taxpayers Association, 41, 45–46, 62–63

Civil Rights Division, 161, 162, 165

Clayton, Joseph, 150

Coalitions
based on common interest, 195–196; understanding the power base for, 195; *See also* Black–white coalitions

Colalillo, Ovid, 71

Colgate High School (Orange), 122

Colgate Park, 203–204

Commissioner of Education, 84

Committee for More Democratic Schools, 42, 45–46, 48–49, 63

Committee for Negro Progress, 158

Committee on Government Contracts, 27, 29

Community Affairs Department, 168, 172

Community Mobilization Center, 160

Compulsory Education Act (1905), 122

Congress of Industrial Organizations (CIO), 8

Congress of Racial Equality, 160

construction industry. *See* building trades

Cook, Bill, 79, 90, 91, 144, 183

Corner of Good Hope (Orange), 93, 145

Cosby, John, 144

CRG (Committee for Representative Government) [later Citizens for Representative Government]
Amalgamated Organizations for Good Government work with, 142–144; building trade training program established by, 98–99; establishment of the, 54; fighting for increased Black representation, 70–82, 88–95, 97, 142, 145–147, 180–181; building trade training program established by, 98–99; fighting gerrymandering and to end school segregation, 84–87, 116–120; seeking coalitions to improve education for all, 116–120, 127–155; *See also* Black leadership; Thompson, Ernie

Crockett, George, Jr., 35

Cronk, Leonard, 133

Crowley, Robert, 149, 152

Crusade for Learning (Newark), 158, 175–178

Danzig, Louis, 160, 165

Davis, William Howe, 47, 81
Day, Janeice, 180–181
DeMaio, Ernie, 190, 191
Democratic Party, 8–9, 70–74, 92, 194–201, 202
Department of Parks and Public Property, 142
DeRosa, Vincent, 144, 147, 148, 152, 153, 155
discrimination. *See* job discrimination; school segregation
D'Italia, Arthur, 146
DiVincentis, Daniel, 128
"Doc." *See* Alexander, John ("Doc")
Doggett, Rebecca, 80, 81, 93, 95*p*, 96, 145, 158, 175, 180, 190, 204, 205
Doll, Ronald, 138–139
Donnelly, Kevin, 182
Donnelly, Susan, 182
Doswell, Morris, 190
drug abuse program (Orange), 203
Dunbar, Paul Laurence, 4
Du Bois, W.E.B., 3

East Ward (Orange), 144, 147, 180, 182, 189
Edgerton, Tom, 190
Education
    Crusade for Learning to promote, 158, 175–178; M.I.T. comprehensive high school report on, 137–138; New Jersey Department of Education report on, 129–130; New Jersey Elementary and Secondary Education Act Title I on, 132–136, 176, 177; *See also* Orange schools
Education Development Association, 139
Elementary and Secondary Education Act Title I [New Jersey], 132–136, 176, 177
Ennis, Evelyn, 63
Episcopal Diocese, 177
Equal Rights for All logo (NNLC), 26*p*
Essex ADA, 160
Essex County Negro Democratic Committee for Recognition, 73

Fair Employment Practices Committee (FEPC), 14, 16, 17–18, 22, 30, 116
Feisner, David, 79
First Presbyterian Church (1741), 207

Fittin, Jim, 92
Fitzgerald, President, 106*p*
Ford River Rouge plant, 21
Franco, Nick, 79, 90–91, 93, 94, 116, 117, 143, 145, 147, 180
Frank, Nathaniel, 136, 137
"freedom schools" (Orange), 118, 127
Freedom Train illustration, 19*p*
Freeway Development Corporation (FDC), 97, 142, 167
Friendship House, 99, 127, 141–142, 186, 203
Fullilove, Mindy Thompson (daughter), 40, 42, 58*p*, 63, 190, 205, 208, 210

Gallagher, John, 63
Garvin, Vicki, 22, 190
Gateway to the South campaign (NNLC), 18, 98
General Motors, 195
gerrymandering school lines
    map of section of Orange showing, 43*p;* Oakwood Avenue School and Central Elementary School, 40–49, 56, 84–87
Give Us This Day Our Daily bread leaflet, 33*p*
Glover, Harvey, 150, 153
Gordon, Larry, 183*p*
government. *See* Orange government
Great Depression, 14
Great Recession (2007), 207
Grimsley, Mildred, 54, 71
Grimsley, Preston, 41, 50, 52*p*, 54, 75–77, 88, 92, 146, 164
Grogan, John, 9
Gulotta, Frances, 19

Hague, Frank ("the Boss"), 8, 10–11, 50, 53, 59, 163
Hansberry, Lorraine, 190
Harmony Bar (Orange), 89
Harris, Earl, 164
Harrison, Jack, 41
Harrison, Mary, 41
Head Start programs, 175
Heckel, Willard, 160, 162, 164
Henry, John, 29
Heywood Avenue School (Orange), 42–49
Higher Achievement Tutoring Program, 124–126

Holland Tunnel construction, 6
Home-Coming Barbecue for Paul Robeson
  leaflet, 57*p*
Hood, Bill, 21, 23, 24–25, 34–35
Horton, Samuel A., 52*p*, 54
House Un-American Activities Committee
  (HUAC), 34–35
housing
  drop-off in Black senior citizens admitted
    to, 203; FDC's proposal to increase Black
    access to, 97–98; Tri-City's work for
    Newark's, 167–174
Housing and Neighborhood Services
  (HANDS), 206, 210
Howard University, 199
Hudson County CIO Council, 103*p*
Hudson County CIO-PAC, 11, 53
Hudson County Industrial Union Council
  (CIO), 11–12
Hughes, Richard J., 149, 162, 164–165

Imperiale, Anthony, 152
Ingram, Rosa Lee, 15
Isaac, Benoit, 41, 45, 45*p*, 46, 52, 71
Isaac, Evelyn, 41, 46, 46*p*, 52, 62
"Is Quality Education Integrated
  Education?" speech (Doc Alexander),
  120
IUE Local 467, 63, 92

Jackson, Bill, 10
Jersey City, 167
Jim Crow practices
  Black labor leadership fighting, 22, 26,
    27, 33, 162; gerrymandering, 41–49,
    56, 83–87; New Day campaign message
    on ending, 64: job discrimination; FEPC's
    work against,14, 16, 17–18, 22, 30;
    fighting for job democracy in Newark,
    158–166; NNLC's work against, 18,
    21–26; protesting against, 28*p*; struggle
    against Jim Crow and, 18, 21–26, 27, 33,
    162; three-party conspiracy of railroad
    industry, 29–30; UE's struggle against,
    16–20; *See also* labor movement;
    Orange school segregation; racism
job equality
  FEPC's work for, 14, 16, 17–18, 22, 30;
    NNLC's campaigns for, 27–33
"Joe Hill" (song), 191

Joey B., 94
John Alexander Association, 70
Johnson, Mordecai, 199–200
Johnson, Yielbonzie, 210
Jones, Benjamin F.
  accomplishments while working to
    improve Orange for all, 99, 148, 153,
    154–155,164–165; election to the Orange
    city council, 88–95; Maggie at campaign
    headquarters for election of, 110*p*; NNLC
    reunion (1970) attended by, 190;
    photographed with Maggie Thompson,
    212*p*, 213*p*; playing on the new bocce
    courts, 112*p*; running again for office
    (1976), 204; speaking at the PACT war
    protest, 186, 187*p*; support for Friendship
    House by, 141–142; supporting Doc's
    school board appointment, 117; Uof O
    practice of "be like Ben," 214; *Walk On
    With Ben* campaign for, 142, 145–147;
    working with key CRG people, 97
Jones–Kelly campaign coalition (1970),
  180–189, 197–198;
Jones–Kelly campaign coalition (1974),
  202
Jones, Carl, 168
Jones–Kelly campaign coalition (1970),
  180–189, 197–198; (1974), 202
Junior Chamber of Commerce, 152

Kahn, Albert E., 200–201
Kaufman, Molly Rose, 207, 215
Kelly, Tom
  campaign leaflet for, 185*p*; running again
    for office (1976), 204; school board
    position held by, 127–128, 147; support
    for new high school by, 153; working as
    attorney for Friendship House, 142
Kennedy, John F., 144*p*, 145
Kennedy, John F. (US president), 48
Kingslow, Harry, 168, 168*p*
Kingslow, Rebecca, 129*p*
Krebs, Paul, 92, 93
Krygar, Clive, 41, 63

Labor-Business-Industry Committee, 138,
  153
labor movement
  FEPC working toward equality, 14, 16,
    17–18, 22, 30; political lessons learned

220

from experiences with, 194–201; struggle against Jim Crow practices in, 22, 26, 27, 33, 41–49, 64, 83–87, 162; *See also* Black workers; job discrimination; white workers
League of Struggle for Negro Rights, 21
League of Women Voters, 103
Legal Services, 186
Leight, Jody, 210
Let Freedom Crash the Gateway to the South campaign (NNLC), 30–33
Let Freedom Ride the Rails (NNLC pamphlet), 30p
Levin-Sagner Homes, 99
Lion, Mr., 62
Local 467, IUE, 63, 92
Locke Insulator strike (Baltimore), 12–13
Lofton, Oliver, 169, 173
Lucarello, Quincy, 144, 147, 148, 153, 155, 188, 203
Lutheran Churches of America, 124

MacFarlane, Jo, 124
Madison Avenue School (Newark), 176–177
Maisich, Henry, 54
Marburger, Carl L., 149
Martinsville Seven, 15
Marzano, Conrad, 144
Mason, Thelma, 41–42
Matthews, Charles, 164
mayor–council reform (1975) [Orange], 203–204
Mazurkiewicz, Paul, 176
McCarthy, Eugene, 182, 206
McCarthyism, 15, 34–35, 37
McGee, Willie, 15
McKim, Mead & White, 207
McLeish, Jim, 117
McIver, Reverend J. Vance, 62
McMillan, Vera B., 168, 204
Meyner, Robert B., 72
Middle States Association, 139
Miles, Jesse, 141
Milligan, John P., 41, 47
Millis, Charles, 53p, 54, 79, 85, 145–146
Mine, Mill and Smelter Workers, 22
Minish, Joseph, 92, 93
M.I.T. comprehensive high school report, 137–138

Monica, John, 143, 153
Montgomery Bus Boycott Proclamation, 107p
Morrissy, Patrick, 206, 207
Mount Auburn (Boston), 207
Murphy, Jim, 41, 183p
Murphy, Marge, 41
Murphy, Ray, 79–81, 88, 90, 118
Murphy's Vote Black policy, 81
Murray, Frank J., 51
Murray, Mrs., 128

NAACP, 84, 85, 86, 88, 89, 118, 165
National Colored Labor Union, 196
National Convention of Negro Elected Officials, 184
National Labor Union, 196
National Negro Labor Council (NNLC) commitment and accomplishments of, 27–33, 198–199; Equal Rights for All logo, 26p ; Gateway campaign (Louisville) by, 98; government attacks against, 34–38, 44; origins and founding convention (1951) of, 18, 21, 22–26, 104p; reunion (1970) of, 111p, 190–193; *See also* Black leadership
Neal, Sterling, 116
Negro Labor Council, 158
The Negro Soldier in World War I, 4
Negro–American Labor Council, 160
Newark Board of Education, 176, 177
Newark College of Engineering (NCE), 159, 160, 161
Newark Coordinating Council (NCC), 158–166, 171
Newark Evening News, 165
Newark Housing Authority, 160
Newark Legal Services, 169
Newark Ministers for Progress, 159
Newark (New Jersey)
Crusade for Learning's work in, 175–178; fighting job discrimination in construction industry, 158–166; *See also* Orange (New Jersey)
Newark Pre-School Council, 175–176
Newark State College, 176
New Day campaign, 54–69, 75, 95–96
New Day for Orange! campaign leaflet, 59p

New Day for Orange–Elect Dr. John W. Alexander leaflet, 68*p*

New Jersey Department of Education report, 129–130, 149, 151

New Jersey Division Against Discrimination (DAD), 41, 47, 48

New Jersey Housing Finance Agency, 168

New York State Committee Against Discrimination, 30

Nixon, Richard, 27, 186

N.J. Advisory Committee to the United States Commission on Civil Rights report (1963), 98

North American Investment Corporation, 173

North Ward (Orange), 144, 152, 203

Oakwood Avenue School (Orange Park), 40–49, 56, 84, 117–120

Oakwood PTA, 45–47, 63

Oliver, Bernadine, 150

Olmstead, Frederick Law, 207

O'Neil, Michael, 153

One Voice for a Democratic Orange campaign, 85–87

Orange Association for Charter Study, 82

Orange city charter, 75–82, 203–204

Orange government
attacks against NNLC by, 34–38, 44; Ben Jones's election to the city council, 88–95; Black–White coalition to increase diversity in, 180–189; CRG referendum for Black representation in, 75–82; lessons learned from Black leadership experiences with, 194–201; mayor–council reform (1975) of, 203–204; McCarthyism within, 15, 34–35, 37, working to change economic policy in, 97–99

Orange Memorial Hospital, 198

Orange Merchants' Association, 152

Orange (New Jersey)
Black leadership challenging the white oligarchy in, 40–58, 73; lessons learned from experiences in, 194–201; postscript to the first edition on outcomes in, 202–205; postscript to the second edition on outcomes in, 206–208; racial tensions of the "hot summer" in, 143; unique

characteristics of, 207; *See also* Newark (New Jersey)

Orange Opportunity Corporation (OOC), 132, 186

Orange school board, 116–120, 139, 195

Orange school desegregation, 117–120

Orange schools
coalitions and programs for improving education for all students, 124–147; Department of Education report on, 129–130; need to build a new high school and long neglect of, 121–131, 137–140; promoting desegregation in, 116–120; segregation of, 41–49, 56, 83–87; *See also* Education

Orange school segregation, 40–49, 56, 83–87. *See also* job discrimination; racism

Orange Senior High School, 130–131, 137–140, 148–155

"Orange's Urgent Educational Needs" pamphlet, 139

Orange Tenants Association, 203

Orange Title I programs, 132–136, 176, 177

Overby, Irving, 154

Overby, Pearl, 90, 91

PACT war protest (Orange Park), 186, 187*p*

Park Avenue School (Orange), 83–84

Parks, Rosa, 107

Peace Movement, 206

politics
lessons from Orange experiences learned about, 194–201; Mordecai Johnson's prophesy on future of the US and, 199–200; seeking power for the powerless, 194; separatist, 197, 200; *See also* Black leadership; Black–white coalitions; white politicians

power
Doc's campaign coalition with labor to build Black, 66–67; helping people to claim their own abilities and, 211; lessons from Orange experiences learned on, 194–201; pig story on being without, 2–3; post-New Day campaign efforts to continue building, 70–74; postscript to the first edition on outcomes of, 202–

205; postscript to the second edition on outcomes of, 206–208; seeking power for the powerless, 194; University of Orange (UofO) for building people's, 207, 210–215; *See also* Black–white coalitions

Prinz, Hilde, 183–184

Prinz, Rabbi Joachim, 183–184

Priorities Investment Corporation, 168–169, 171, 173, 174, 208

Proclamation supporting Montgomery Bus Boycott (UE Women's Conference), 107p

racism
Ernie's hard line regarding, 12–13, 37–38 as response to efforts for change, 26, 34, 82, 148–155; *See also* job discrimination; Orange school segregation

railroad industry, 29–30

Republican party, 77

Robeson, Paul, 25, 55p, 56–58, 191

Rollins, Hazel, 128p, 149–150

Roosevelt, Franklin D., 11, 14, 53, 66

Rutgers Law School, 159, 161–162

Rutgers University Ernie Thompson Archive, 107

Rutgers University study, 139

Ryan, Maso, 204

Sagner, Alan, 99

Santora, Bill, 190

Satori (literary magazine), 150

Savage, Richard, 148, 155

Savage, Walter G., 51

Schmid, Emil A., 151

schools. *See* Orange schools

Sears-Roebuck, 6

separatist politics, 197, 200

Shain, Joel, 183, 184

Sills, Arthur J., 162, 163

Simmons, Charles, 124, 144

slavery history, 4, 196

Smith Act, 21

Smith, Alice, 190

Smith, Bill, 116

Smith, Harold, 190p, 191, 193

Smith, Harry, 41

"Song of Freedom" speech (1951) [Thompson], 23

South Seventeenth Street School (Amity Village), 177

South Ward (Orange), 144, 182–183, 189

Squires, Joe, 116

Stavis, Morton, 97–98, 190

Strong Men concept (New Day campaign), 61–62, 65–66

Stubbs, William, 164

Study Help program, 124

Subversive Activities Control Board (SACB), 34, 36

Sutton, Percy, 184

Taylor, Gladys, 141

Teamster Local 97, 94

Texile Workers, 19

Thomas, Morris ("Shorty"), 183

Thomas, Rudy, 63, 64, 92, 188p–189

Thompson, Emma (first wife), 7

Thompson, Ernie
answer to "Who is you?" by, 1; arrested with Charles Millis, 145–146; on children's right to live and work, 115; on commitment of Black labor leadership by, 39; directing resolution for new high school from hospital bed, 148; early experience in union organizing, 5–13; "Homeboy" or "Home" nickname of, 1, 49; on learning to live together, 215; legacy to the next generation of organizers by, 207–208; Maryland boyhood of, 3–4; "Old Man" poem read by, 95–96; origins of "Big Train" nickname of, 22; photographs of, 102p, 103p, 104p,105p, 106p, 109p, 111p, 183p; "Song of Freedom" speech (1951) by, 23; wishing for world with *laughter of children,* 201; *See also* Black leadership; CRC (Committee for Representative Government) [later Citizens for Representative Government]; *Homeboy Came to Orange* (Thompson and Fullilove)

Thompson, Jennie (mother), 3

Thompson, Joshua (father), 2, 3–4

Thompson, Joshua Paul (son), 109p

Thompson, Maggie (second wife), 40–41, 105p, 110p, 111p, 150–151, 204, 209, 212p, 213p

Thompson, Mindy (daughter), *See* Fullilove, Mindy Thompson (daughter)

Thompson, Philip Henry (grandfather), 4

Title I (Elementary and Secondary
Education Act) [New Jersey], 132–136,
176, 177
To Be Young, Gifted and Black (Hansberry), 190
Trade Union Convention (1950), 19–20, 21
Transcript (Orange newspaper), 42–45, 47,
75–76, 83, 88–89,
Travis, Maurice, 22
Trenton Six, 15
Tri-City Citizens Union for Progress, 158,
167–174, 204–205
Tri-City Economic Union No. 1, 168
Tri-City People's Center, 174, 204
Turner, Irvine, 158, 164
Tuskegee Airmen, 22

UE (United Electrical, Radio and Machine
Workers of America)
Black caucus and leadership in, 15–16;
Eastern Metal members of, 19–20;
government attacks against NNLC and,
34–38; origins and early work of, 8, 12,
14; Proclamation supporting Montgomery
Bus Boycott during Women's Conference,
107*p*; strike supporting women's equality,
108*p*; struggle against job discrimination
by, 16–20, 37–38; Thompson's work and
time with, 8, 12, 14, 16–20, 37–38; *See
also* CIO (Congress of Industrial
Organization); unions
Uncle Tom's Cabin, 4
Union Baptist Church (Orange), 62, 84
union organizing
Ernie's early lessons on, 5–9; Ernie's
legacy to the next generation of, 207–208
unions
Black workers forming their own, 196–
197; Ernie's early experiences with, 5–9
evolution of Black leadership in, 5–13, 18,
21–26; exclusion of Blacks from white,
14, 16, 98, 196–197; *See also specific union*
union strikes, 7–8, 12–13, 108*p*
United Auto Workers (UAW), 21
United Brothers, 152
United States
current crossroads facing the, 200;
Mordecai Johnson's prophecy about,
199–200
University of Orange (UofO), 207,
210–215

Upsala College, 124
Up The Programmatic Tree illustration
(Brown), 55*p*
up the programmatic tree story, 54–56
Urban League, 160
Urcoli, Eugene, 203

Vietnam War, 186, 206
Vote Black policy, 81

Wagner Act, 8
Walk On With Ben (CRG), 142, 145–147
Ward, Eulis C. ("Honey"), 73, 164
Warner, William, 150
Washington-Dodd Urban Renewal Project,
98
Way, Herb, 110, 112, 113
Wayne County CIO, 22
Wells, Karen, 210
West Ward (Orange), 144, 189
Wheatley, Phyllis, 4
white politicians
Black leadership challenging the Orange
oligarchy of, 50–58; challenging
gerrymandering school lines practice of,
41–49; Charter Change Association
coalition between CRG and, 77–82; *See
also* Black–white coalitions; politics
White, Charles, xviii, 33
White, Reverend Russell, 153
white women, 18–20.
See also Black women
white workers, 5–9, 15–17. *See also* labor
movement
Williams, Donna, 214–215
Williams, Doris, 204
Williams, Earl, 190
Williams, Madeline, 164
Winans, Derek, 161
women's movement, 192–193
Woody, Colson, 71, 88, 116, 168
World War II, 14, 16

Ylivisaker, Paul, 151
Young, Coleman ("Big Red"), 21–22, 29–
30, 32, 34–35, 104*p*, 111*p*, 179, 190, 192;
Youth Helping Youth, 177

Zisman, Milton A., 139, 204